Sales Management: Developing the skills of the sales team

All about training, coaching, mentoring, formal sales qualifications, and other opportunities for personal development (including for the Sales Manager).

Tim Royds

MA(Sales Management), Dip (Sales), FInstSMM, FCIM, BSc(Hons)

The author can be contacted both via highclere's web site www.highcleresales.com, and / or the e-mail address of hello@highcleresales.com .

First edition
Published December 2016
ISBN: 978-1539634867

All references to website addresses and other virtual resources are correct at time of publishing

Contents

List of figures

List of tables

The 9 Books in the 'Sales Management' series:

1. What it's really all about
What Sales Management really means and the activities to concentrate on to ensure that the sales team *make success happen!*

2. So now you're a Sales Manager...
The do's and don'ts when first appointed to the role.

3. Developing the skills of the sales team
All about training, coaching, mentoring, formal sales qualifications, and other opportunities for personal development (including for the Sales Manager).

4. Field Based Coaching
Avoiding the parachute visit (*"...thought I'd just drop in!"*) and moving instead to a structured coaching focused day which builds skills and confidence.

5. Motivational Sales Meetings
Ensuring that they're productive and that they're the ones the team *look forward* to attending.

6. Leading the sales team
Motivating, engaging, and inspiring the team to drive towards the Vision... very much a case of '*lighting the fire within*'!

7. Recruitment & Selection
How to ensure you hire the Winners rather than the also-rans.

8. Internal sales teams
Addressing the challenges specific to office based sales teams and contact centres.

9. Sales Planning
How Winners create the future as they want it.

Preface to the Series

There's no doubt that the key driving force behind successful sales teams is the Sales Manager. Throughout my career I've observed how the appointment of a new Sales Manager can change the fortunes of a sales team - same salespeople, same roles being managed, same products, same customers, and same market place – but the different Sales Manager achieves different results. Sometimes of course this unfortunately is not for the better!

Clearly though, there must be some things that the more successful Sales Managers do differently. And surely it makes good sense to understand what these things are so that these more successful approaches, strategies, and tactics can be used by others?

The success that high quality Sales Management generates is the lifeblood of organisations. No sales means no production, or in the service sector idle service providers. A sustained flow of orders though means that production, distribution, and all other parts of the organisation have the fuel they need to work. A sustained flow of profitable sales provides the income for companies to employ staff, invest in research & development, invest in new technology, provide training – and all this and more underpins the company's ability to be competitive and successful in the future – and so sustain the flow of orders and profits. Successful and profitable companies drive the economy, and via the payment of taxes fund public sector jobs and the many services that support the more needy in society. Sales success driven by proven, high quality, Sales Management practices is obviously a laudable goal to strive for.

From the point of view of individual salespeople and Sales Managers, sales success means recognition, increased earnings, and faster career progression.

Sales success makes organisations great places to be too. Future employment is secure, personal stress is reduced, and the general 'feel' of the 'place' (be that a specific geographical location or virtual) is a lot more vibrant.

If only there were a magic formula which provided the simple 'know-how' that underpins all this success!

Well of course there is no simple formula… there is no simple 'you do this, then you do this, then that creates success'. The role is too complex for this. There are though recognised tools, principles, and approaches that we know most definitely work, and which of them to use, when to use them, and how to use them depends on the circumstances. This is why what's needed today is Sales Managers who have the ability to think issues through, and the capability to understand which tools, strategies, approaches and principles can be called upon to help - depending on the circumstances.

However, it's difficult to decide which tool to pull out of the box and how best to use it if it isn't in the tool box in the first place! The purpose of this entire series of books is to provide exactly this… the tools, principles and know-how which underpin success.

Over the course of my career I've enjoyed the privilege of working with and meeting an enormous number of Sales Managers. Some I reported to when I held roles as a salesperson in the early part of my career. Many I've worked with in my role as a consultant and trainer. Some of these were already experienced and successful, and others were inexperienced and still in the process of understanding and learning about this challenging role. I've even had the opportunity to judge the 'Sales Leader of the Year' category of the UK National Sales Awards. I've learned from them all though. In particular I've been able to observe first-hand how 'text book' Sales Management can be implemented practically and pragmatically, and what really does produce the desired results in the *real* world.

Recognising that first-hand observations are valid, I'm also conscious that there is far too much material published in both hard and soft copy from what I cynically refer to as 'the school of it's a well known fact' – and which repeats and reinforces selling myths that simply aren't true. So as well as my own observations, the material in this book series is backed up by objective studies and surveys. Most of the books also include at least one Case Study which describes an organisation which has put into practice the principles discussed in that book, and have achieved significantly as a consequence.

It would be remiss of me if I didn't recognise how my thinking has been influenced by studying for the Diploma in Professional Sales via the Chartered Institute of Marketing, and the Masters Degree in Strategic Sales Management via the Business School of Portsmouth University (I am now one of the Course Directors who teaches on the former, and guest speak on the latter). These qualifications certainly provided me with knowledge. More importantly though, they developed in me the discipline to question everything, and to never accept statements of 'fact' at face value, but to always ask: "...*where is the proof for that?*" It's the participation in these high level programmes that has also contributed to the motivation for me to contribute to Sales Management literature – and to contribute material that is robust, up to date, and if used for guidance will indeed drive the achievement of impressive results.

The material is presented as a series of individual 'bite sized' books, each of which can be read as a 'stand alone' item. I chose to adopt this approach rather than produce just one large text for a number of reasons...

- This allows readers to acquire the information and know-how that's most relevant to the specifics of their role. Field Based Coaching is a fundamental and absolutely critical part of the Field Sales Manager's role, but of little relevance to the Sales Manager who leads an office based team, for example.
- They're a lot easier to carry around! ...so good for people who like to read 'on the move'.
- It makes purchasing a lot more cost-effective; readers can simply purchase precisely what they want without the need to spend money on any superfluous material.

Finally, I must thank the many Sales Managers and other respected contacts who commented on the initial outline notes I developed for this book series when first embarking on the project. They are people I've known for many years and have a high respect for. I simply asked: "*Is this right?*. I value both the encouragement I received, their thoughts & input regarding points I needed to include, and their guidance on what they felt was particularly important. This input has ensured that the books are not only thorough and robust, but also practical and pragmatic – and relevant to Sales Managers today.

Preface to "Sales Management: Developing the skills of the sales team"

It's been interesting how writing this third book of the series has evolved into a bigger and longer-term project than I'd originally anticipated...

It's certainly challenging to make rapid progress writing at the same time as managing 'business as usual' in my role as B2B sales consultant and trainer – prospecting, meeting prospects, developing proposals, account managing, and of course consultancy, coaching and training. In busy periods, it's been the writing that's had to take a lower priority.

As well as the time management challenges, it's been interesting to see how the volume of information and practical ideas I planned to provide has grown. I guess this should be no surprise really as people development is an absolute passion of mine, and is what my career focus has been since founding my consultancy business back in 2000 and indeed before that too.

My first ever role as a sales training specialist in all honesty came about through necessity rather than because of a conscious effort to move my career in that direction. As a salesperson in the pharmaceutical industry, my goal was to move into Regional Sales Management, and whilst it wasn't 'officially' the recognised career pathway, what normally happened was that people moved into a training role as a 'stepping stone' along the way. So it seemed to me that this was a good idea for me too, though I saw the move as a necessary but temporary side-ways step.

My time as an internal sales trainer though proved to be rather successful. It was very enjoyable too! This was where I learned what I regarded at the time as the fundamentals of training. I didn't appreciate though how much higher the standards within the pharmaceutical industry were compared to other sectors. So the idea of attending a two-part training programme on 'Criterion Referenced Instruction' (about how to define training objectives and design training interventions), each of which was a whole week in duration, I thought was normal - as I didn't have anything to compare this experience to. For the same reason, I also thought that the robust standards that we applied to training & development *per se* were normal. The fact that I wasn't allowed to coach until I'd attended a two-day course on the subject and demonstrated to the satisfaction of the course director that I could apply the principles to given standards seemed to me to be simply sensible, and certainly, I assumed, not different to what any other organisation did. I now realise that the standards were high, and the disciplines admirable.

I also went on to hold the role of field-based sales coach for around 12 months, and then learned more about the practical applications of what I'd been teaching on sales training courses in the real world. There is certainly a science to this activity – as is described in the soon to be published fourth book of this series... "Sales Management: Field Based Coaching".

I really learned about the pragmatics of training though when I moved into the role or Regional Sales Manager. Having arrived there from a training stable, my belief was that 'training' was the way to success. It was not long however, before I realised that even after having provided the most sophisticated and advanced training possible, what really mattered was how people felt when the alarm went off in the morning.

So yes, this book is a summary (though a rather long summary!) of what I've learned over the years about developing sales people. My aim has been to focus on what really works, not by sharing information from what I often refer to (cynically!) as 'the school of it's a well-known fact', but sharing what we know from objective studies makes Training & Development effective. It is though written not from the purely theoretical standpoint, it's written from the point of view of practicality and pragmatics – it's about what I've learned in the real world about the practical application of what objectives studies have proven to work. It's written from the point of view of answering the question: "*What would I do now, and how would I do these things if I was a Sales Manager?*"

So in terms of reading this book, then the primary target is Sales Managers. Why I believe that an understanding of how to grow and develop people is so important and relevant to Sales Managers will become apparent as you read its content. It doesn't take a genius though to work out that a sales team with high ability, skills, and know-how is more desirable than one with low ability, skills, and know-how.

Sales training specialists should enjoy the content of the book too. It is indeed written from the point of view of the Sales Manager, but since this role is their primary customer, shouldn't this be the way that sales training specialists are thinking about implementing their role?!

And finally, the book is highly relevant to generic training specialists and those in Human Resources with responsibility for training. Whilst issues such as 'coaching', 'training needs analysis' and 'maximising returns from training and development' are relevant to all parts of the business, the discussion about how to apply these to the world of sales will inform their ability to speak in the language of their Sales Manager customers, and indeed to their sales professional customers *per se*.

About the Author
Tim Royds

MA(Sales Management), Dip (Sales), FInstSMM, FCIM,
BSc(Hons)

Tim is a highly experienced sales consultant, sales trainer, and sales coach.

He began his sales career in the pharmaceutical industry in 1982, having gained a degree in Applied Biology. Initially beginning his apprenticeship as a 'GP representative', Tim followed the 'classic' career pathway of Hospital Sales specialist, Internal Sales Training specialist, Field Sales Training specialist and then Regional Sales Manager. During this period he enjoyed 'Top Ten' success as a representative, many accolades as a Training specialist and as Sales Manager led his team to Number one position during a pioneering product launch.

In 1993 Tim moved into the role of Sales Training and Development Manager with Barclays Mercantile, (specialists in business-to-business finance), and as a result of successes here was asked to also support the selling efforts of a number of other B2B Business Units within the Barclays Group.

In 2001 Tim moved to independent consultancy, and formed the company *highclere*. He's now worked with a wide range of industries and organisations, including Amadeus, Bahrain Telecommunications, Barclays, the BBC, Deloitte & Touche, Glaxo, SG Equipment Finance, Sprint Corporation, Steris, and Working Links. To date, he has facilitated events in 29 countries of 5 different continents, attended by delegates from 91 different countries.

Tim has a passion for professionalism and the achievement of high standards throughout both the Sales and Sales Training professions. To that end he was a committee member of the Sales Training Association (now Sales Performance Association) 1996-2006 (Chairman 1998-2003) and has judged the National Sales Awards each year since their inception in 1996. He is also a Course Director in the Global Delivery Framework of the Chartered Institute of Marketing (CIM) and an experienced deliverer of the CIM Certificate, Advanced Certificate and Diploma in Professional Sales.

Tim was one of the first six people in the UK to achieve the Masters Degree in Strategic Sales Management from the Business School of Portsmouth University, having previously completed the CIM Diploma in Professional Sales. He now speaks on the MA programme, specialising in *The Use of Positioning Strategies in Professional Sales*, and *Branding*. He has also spoken on the BA Business & Management programme of Winchester University on the subject of Key Account Management.

Tim was an active member of the Marketing and Sales Standards Setting Body (MSSSB), a UK government sponsored body which first developed the National Occupational Standards in Sales. The framework and content of these now underpin all UK Sales Qualifications. He has also achieved Fellowship status of both the CIM and Institute of Sales and Marketing Management.

He has also written numerous articles for various sales journals and magazines including "Winning Edge", the bi-monthly magazine of the Institute of Sales & Marketing Management, and has also been asked to provide 'expert comment' on the issue of 'sales techniques' for "Which" the magazine of the UK Consumer's Association.

Foreword

I have been involved in sales for most of my working life, firstly as a salesperson moving into management, and then into training and development. So I hope I have a comprehensive understanding of sales in all it's different guises.

I have known Tim since 1997 and have always admired his approach. He is recognised as an expert in the sales arena and has great communicative skills, whilst sharing his knowledge, skills and experiences.

Tim's approach to this book is quite refreshing as it is written in a way that is easy to follow and talks a lot of sense. The sales team in today's business world is under more pressure than ever to meet targets – numbers, product/service mix and profit, all to appease stake and shareholders.

All sales teams are a mix of personalities, ages, backgrounds and, more importantly, have different motivators driving them to achieve their goals. When considering how to develop the skills of **your** sales team, there are a lot of key answers in this book that will help focus on structuring as to how to plan and prioritise your resources. The balance between skills / knowledge / attitude is very relevant, and this book gives a very good insight into how attitude is as important, if not more, to the success and confidence to individuals in the team.

All sales team development is not necessarily about training courses, as Tim so rightly recognises, but about coaching and mentoring, which this book provides an understanding of with great insight, and in a structured and informative style.

Tim's book is not only good for new Sales Managers, but also a very good refresher for the experienced Sales Manager who believes they have been there and have the full wardrobe. I certainly had a lot of reality checks whilst reading it.

As well as this book being a great aide memoire, the **key thought** sections alone are worth reading regularly to give focus on areas you have possibly identified for improvement.

This book has the potential to save the Sales Manager and his team... time, resources and money! And, as a business proposition, that is very saleable.

Peter Cooksley
Chairman, Sales Performance Association

1. Introduction & some key considerations

Assuming that the right people have been employed in the sales team in the first place, that everyone in the sales team enjoys high levels of role clarity (as discussed in the first book in this series: "Sales Management: What it's *really* all about"), and in particular absolute clarity regarding the quantity and quality of activities required for success, then the Sales Manager has only three other key issues to focus on:

1) Does each person have the skills and knowledge required to execute the required Inputs successfully and efficiently? and...

2) ...do they have a high drive and desire to do these things? and...

3) ...do they enjoy high levels of confidence and self-belief?

The second question is about motivation and engagement, which is discussed in some depth in book No.6 of this series ("Sales Management: Leading the sales team"). It's certainly worth making the point here though that skill development and the building of an environment which provides the opportunity for personal growth will have a positive effect on these critical issues.

The third question is about something that's very intangible. But isn't it massively important? In sport you will no doubt have seen on numerous occasions how a lack of confidence and self-belief has drastically impacted on performance. And indeed on other occasions how an individual blessed with high levels

1

of confidence and self-belief has performed exceptionally well. It's often said that "...*they played above themselves*" – which is utter nonsense of course, because you can't play better than you can play! What's actually being said is that something special has happened which has enabled them to play to an even higher standard than is normally the case, and at a standard which is near, if not at, the maximum of their capabilities. And that special something is normally related to 'mind-set'.

This is why discussion focused on 'Developing the skills of the sales team', needs to include consideration of how to elevate levels of confidence and self-belief too. Of course, training that enhances skills will in itself help, as *knowing* that you have the skills and knowledge required to succeed helps to generate the *belief that you can* succeed. None the less, the issue of how to develop confidence in each salesperson in the team will be revisited from time to time as we consider how skills and knowledge can be acquired and embedded, in order that they drive the selling habits that underpin the attainment of success.

> **Key thought: How much consideration is given to building the inner belief that "...*I can*" in your sales team?**

So whilst this book concentrates on the first of these three questions, its content cannot be seen in isolation from the other two of them. The nine books in this series consider issues separately to make their content more 'digestible', and so that readers can focus on the subjects that are most relevant to them personally. All the issues the series discusses though are inextricably linked.

Since the quantity and quality of Outputs produced by the sales team are directly related to the quantity and in particular the quality of Inputs they put in, and the quantity and quality of the Inputs is directly related to each person's ability, then ensuring that the sales team has high levels of ability *must* be considered to be a high priority Sales Management activity.

You need quality material in the first place...

It is true that you can't make a Stradivarius violin out of a piece of old chipboard; to make a Stradivarius (or more accurately speaking to make a new violin to the same quality standards as a Stradivarius) you need to begin with high quality material in the first place. The same is true for sales teams. When building sales teams, acquiring 'quality material' means employing the right people with the innate qualities and attributes required for the role. And having acquired quality

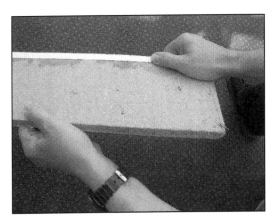

figure 1. "You can't make a Stradivarius out of a piece of old chipboard"

3

material, this then needs to be crafted properly – which means carefully, with the right tools, at the right speed, and in the right way. Once fully formed, then the final product needs to be constantly cared for and polished, lest it deteriorate with the ravages of time. All this is just as true of high quality salespeople as it is of a high quality musical instrument.

The Stradivarius analogy though is also misleading, because provided you have the right material it's theoretically possible to hire in an expert craftsman to make the violin for you. As a Sales Manager though, you can't hire someone to come in and do the entire Sales Management job for you. Some Sales Managers can call on support from colleagues who are specialists in the area of sales training, and so who can help with and support the development process. There is the opportunity to bring in external consultancy expertise too. Even when bringing in expertise to help though, it remains the Sales Manager who has the responsibility of orchestrating these activities, and who has a significant role to play themselves when following-up and coaching what's learned (as we'll discuss in chapters 3. and 4.)

That's why this book, although focused on 'Developing the skills of the sales team', is not targeted specifically at Sales Training Specialists. For the Sales Manager to be able to manage the development of their team effectively, they need to understand the principles that underpin this important subject - and that's what this book provides. Having said that, the content is though just as applicable to those whose role is *totally* focused on sales team development.

Ability to learn…

Two of the attributes and qualities that contribute to an individual salesperson being 'quality material' are:
1) their ability to learn, and
2) their appetite for learning.

Ability to learn relates to how easily and quickly an individual can acquire new skills, and comprehend, absorb, and apply information (product, competitor product, customer knowledge, market knowledge, etc.) This is not necessarily the same as having an appetite to learn – which is about the desire to learn and grow as a professional; it's possible unfortunately for a salesperson to have the ability to learn, but not a high drive to do so.

When employed as a Regional Manager in the pharmaceutical industry, 'ability to learn' was one of the core competencies I looked for during the Recruitment & Selection process – and with good reason…

At that time, the UK National Health Service (NHS) was not gradually evolving… it was changing massively and very rapidly, and for the first time was being managed via the application of business principles. Health care professionals (our customers) were being challenged to change the way they thought – from being focused pretty well totally on treating and preventing illness, to also taking responsibility for budgets and allocating resources in the most effective way possible - for example negotiating which hospital services were going to be used from which hospital, what the cross-charged price of these services was going to be, etc. In short, they were being asked to think more like business people.

Before this time, the 'perfect fit' salesperson for this environment was someone with a nursing background or life science degree, as they already had some knowledge of physiology, could readily understand the challenges of a healthcare professional, and were already familiar with scientific language and terminology.

The environment though was changing massively. This did not alter the need of pharmaceutical salespeople to understand the challenges of the customer. What *had* changed though was what these challenges were. So now the ideal salesperson for my team was someone who understood the business related challenges of the customer, but could also enjoy a medical focused discussion about the products we promoted, how they worked, benefits and drawbacks for the patient, etc. I believed that it was easier to teach science to someone with a business focused mind-set, than it was to teach business mind-set to someone with a scientific background.

My ideal candidate profile therefore changed from someone with a nursing background or life science degree, to someone with a business related degree qualification who had the ability to learn, and an appetite to do so. A degree level qualification was good evidence that they had the ability to learn and so could acquire the medical know-how required to do the job successfully. During the selection process this is exactly what I looked for, and I'm pleased to say that the appointments I made taking that approach were indeed the right ones - the graduates I employed were successful, and achieved an on-target level of performance very quickly.

The Job Purpose of a Sales Manager is to *achieve sales through others*, and the sales team's ability to *achieve sales* is underpinned by them having the required skills and knowledge. If they don't have the full complement of skills and knowledge to the highest possible standards, then these pieces of skill and knowledge need to be acquired. And the salesperson needs to be able to acquire them.

> **Key thought: It's important that the individuals who the Sales Manager employs in the sales team have the ability to grow, to take on board new information, and to develop new skills. The more they can develop and grow, the more they will achieve. To what degree is this considered during the Recruitment & Selection process?**

Moreover, how customers buy continues to change and evolve, which means in turn that the sales process is likely to continually evolve too. That's why the skills and knowledge that are required to execute todays sales process are not necessarily the same as those that were needed in the past. So not only is the initial development of skills and knowledge and so growth of the salesperson important, their ongoing and continual development is important too.

Putting all this together explains why I recommend that amongst the attributes looked for during the Recruitment and Selection process are:
1) an ability to learn, and
2) an appetite for learning.

Generation Y

The term 'Generation Y' is given to those born between the early 1980's and the early 2000's. The previous generation to this was known as 'Generation X', and not surprisingly the subsequent one 'Generation Z'! Not every generation is designated by a letter though; I am part of the so called 'Baby Boomer' generation, who were born between the mid 1940's and mid 1960's.

Saying that a particular generation begins and ends on a specific year is artificial of course; one generation merges into another and there is no absolute black and white. These terms can though be helpful in providing an understanding of the different drivers and motivators that different generations have, which impact in turn on what management and leadership style is going to be most appropriate. And there are indeed differences between generations, some of which are quite significant. More is explored about this in Book 6. of this series, "Sales Management: Leading the Sales Team". This brief section focuses on some of the issues which impact on the management of Generation Y's training and development.

Before discussing how Generation Y differs to previous generations and how their differences might impact on their training and development, it's important to recognise that there is as much difference between individual people within each generation as there is between different generations. It's essential that individual salespeople are treated as exactly that: individuals. That's why it's important that Sales Managers invest time to understand each salesperson's specific development needs, and to also understand what the most appropriate means of supporting each salesperson's personal development are. One size does not necessarily fit all. This brief review of some of the recognised differences between Generation Y and other generations is intended to highlight just one or two issues that should influence the Sales Manager's thought processes.

For Sales Managers reading this who *are* of Generation Y, it's equally true that you need to be aware that the more mature members of your sales team may not necessarily have the same perceptions as you do. So when engineering the working environment for them that they will find motivational, don't assume that they want the same as you do.

Perhaps the obvious first place to begin discussion about generational differences is with the use of technology. Generation Y is more familiar and comfortable with technology than any of their previous generations; use of computers, the Internet, and smart phones is second nature to them. Because of their comfort with technology, there is often a natural assumption that their preferred way of learning is via technology and so e-learning resources of some description. In fact, this isn't true. A research report(1) published in 2015 by the Chartered Institute of Personnel & Development (cipd) showed that they are actually no more focused on e-learning than previous generations. Quite why this is, the authors of this report suggest, is open to speculation. There is a suggestion that the underlying cause might be that their expectations regarding technology are very high, and that they quickly lose patience with any e-learning materials that are deemed to be below standard or even regarded as basic. And expectations do tend to be high, driven by the high quality of computer games and Internet sited resources that they are used to.

> **Key thought: Just because a given generation is very technologically savvy, it doesn't necessarily mean that this is their preferred way of learning. Remember that to assume makes an <u>ass</u> out of <u>u</u> and <u>me</u>!**

The overall message on this issue is very clear though: Don't assume that Generation Y wants or prefers to learn via e-based resources or other technology. And the message to Generation Y Sales Managers is that if you're not keen on e-learning resources, don't assume that your more mature colleagues feel the same as you do; they may actually prefer them!

Generation Y's perceptions regarding the purpose of learning and why it's useful to them certainly can be a little different to other generations. Two key drivers influence these perceptions...

The first of these are their expectations that their job will provide a good work/life balance; indeed, this is one of the top five most important things this generation tends to look for from their job(2). The mind-set of this generation is more towards working to live rather than living to work(3), which can be a little different to Sales Managers of other generations.

The second is Generation Y's mentality that their career path is likely to move them from one organisation to another. Some have interpreted this as meaning that this generation lacks loyalty. It's been claimed though that this is more about them having been brought up in a period of uncertainty when many large and previously perceived to be 'solid' organisations, have simply disappeared. Putting all this together means that to Generation Y, the key purpose of learning is to enable them to achieve more in *the role they have today*, and not necessarily about preparing them for potential roles in the future. After all, with such uncertainty about what their future is going to be, how is it possible to prepare for it? Achieving more now though can increase security (and so reduce uncertainty), and a track record of success will provide a good foundation for the future too.

Such a mind-set is different to previous generations who, generally speaking, viewed personal development as a means of preparing themselves for future senior roles in their current organisation. For Sales Managers, this means being aware that Generation Y salespeople may not be motivated by the development of skills for roles in the long-term future, and it certainly means that the purpose and benefits of training & development need to be articulated in a way that's aligned to their 'in the present' motivations. This is more about articulating immediate value than it is about helping the Generation Y salesperson develop a Vision for their future.

Key thought: To what degree do you take into consideration the different motivations of different generations when discussing with an individual their aspirations, and the personal development which will enable these aspirations to be achieved?

Another difference of this generation to previous ones are their expectations related to the speed at which promotions are achieved. They are expected to happen a lot faster. This expectation provides the Sales Manager with a dilemma... On the one hand, it's important to ensure that there are realistic expectations regarding how quickly promotions are going to be won; a Sales Manager who is perceived to have 'over promised, and under-delivered' will have created an environment which encourages the salesperson to leave the organisation. Equally, communicating a message that promotion is going be slower than the salesperson would like could also lead to them wanting to leave! So there's a tricky balance to be achieved here, and the advice I would offer would be to constantly provide Generation Y employees with new and fresh challenges that will provide them the opportunity to succeed and so build up a track record of success. Though having said that, this is not a bad approach to managing any member of any sales team anyway.

What Generation Y most certainly expect is support and help so that they can 'achieve more today'. So in terms of Sales Manager behaviours, this means mentoring and coaching in order to support this – and both these development activities will be considered later on.

How people learn

The process that people move through as they learn is summarised by the diagram in figure 1. (adapted from Kolb's Learning Cycle(4)). To explain how this works, let's consider a theoretical scenario: a face-to--face meeting between a salesperson and a customer, where the salesperson is promoting a newly launched piece of industrial machinery…

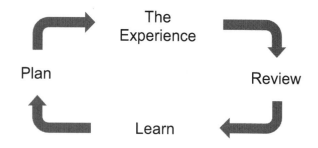

The
Experience

Plan

Review

Learn

figure 2. The Learning Cycle

Here, first of all, is a description of one part of **the experience**…

Part way through the conversation, the customer raises a concern about price. Before answering, the salesperson initially asks questions to clarify precisely what's 'behind' the concern, and establishes that the concern isn't so much about the actual price, but about the initial deposit that needs to be paid. They also uncover that the customer is approaching the end of their financial year, and that they have very limited cash resources left to invest in any new or upgraded machinery. As a consequence of understanding this underlying reason behind the concern, the salesperson empathises with the customer's situation, and then goes on to explain how invoicing can be arranged in order that invoice and payment dates fall into the following financial year rather than this current one, and which means that the machinery can be acquired now, but paid for out of the following financial year's budget. The salesperson then checks to establish how comfortable the customer feels with the response that's been provided, and the customer not only replies positively, but also immediately goes on to provide a number of buying signals. These the salesperson responds to, and as a consequence successfully gains a commitment to purchase.

Following the meeting, the salesperson invests time to **review** what happened. This **review** is likely to include what happened when the customer raised the concern about price… what exactly the customer said, how the salesperson responded (both verbally and non-verbally), and whether or not this elicited a positive response from the customer.

In this example, the customer's response was clearly positive, which indicates that what the salesperson did (the Inputs) were appropriate to this particular situation. Thinking this through in order to identify

13

precisely what was done to achieve the desired result achieves **learning**, as does consideration of other situations where the same approach is likely to be appropriate, or indeed inappropriate.

This will lead to the conscious **planning** of what to do in similar circumstances in the future – so helping the salesperson to increase the quality of their future Inputs, which will lead in turn to an enhancement of their Outputs, and so increase the Sales Manager's ability *to achieve sales through others*.

A detailed review of the meeting with the customer might also include parts of the meeting that were *less* positive. For example, it might be that at one point the customer said "*I didn't realise that you were going to be providing me information about this new piece of machinery. It would have been useful for me to have my production manager here so he could have heard from you first-hand how this is going to help us with the new contract we've just won. I'll be able to pass this information on myself, but as I'm out of the office now until next week this will cause a bit of a delay.*"

Reviewing what the customer said should lead to the salesperson identifying that this is going to impact negatively on how quickly the sale is going to be achieved. The question of how this could have been better managed, or even better prevented altogether, then needs to be addressed. Thinking through the potential solutions enables **learning**. There is likely to be a realisation that an agenda for the meeting should have been sent in advance, so that the customer had a clear understanding of the purpose of the meeting and what was going to be discussed. This would have alerted the customer to the fact that the meeting was to include the presentation of information about a new piece of machinery, and so prompt the thought that the production manager would benefit from attending the meeting too. There might also have been further benefits, such as a reduced chance of the customer postponing and rescheduling the meeting – which they might have done had they not realised how important and significant it was.

So having **reviewed** the experience, and thought through the alternative approaches they could have taken, the salesperson will have **learned**. They can then **plan** to ensure that they send a proposed outline in advance of meetings in the future.

Beginning this description of how the learning cycle works with a positive example is very deliberate. Learning is not just about identifying what's been done either not quite 'right' or even 'wrong' altogether. Rather, it's about understanding how to be more effective in the role via all experiences. So yes, it certainly does mean thinking through carefully what happened and why these things happened after an unsuccessful sales meeting - but that is *only one* sort of experience that can be learned from. Learning by reviewing successes is equally, if not more important. The more the salesperson understands what it is that they are doing which achieves the desired results, the more consciously they can do these things in the future.

> **Key thought: The ratio 70:20:10 is often quoted to represent how employees learn... 70% comes via experience, 20% via social learning with colleagues, and 10% via formal training events and training materials such as e-learning.**

The two examples provided also reinforce an important point about learning, growing, and developing the skills of the sales team. Attending training courses is not the only way that people learn;

learning by doing the day-to-day job in itself is a learning opportunity, and probably one of the most important learning methods that there is.

Implications for the Sales Manager...

The critical issue that's driven from an understanding of the learning cycle, is that people learn via the reviewing of experiences.   Now whilst this might sound rather like stating the obvious, it means that without the reviewing part, learning isn't going to take place, and reviewing requires an investment of conscious thought and time.

The world of professional sales has never been a more busy, hectic, and pressured place than it is today. It's all too easy for a field based salesperson to have a working day where a meeting with a customer is completed, the CRM system is updated, and the challenge then is to race off to the next appointment with the hope that there will be no unexpected traffic delays along the way. They arrive for the next appointment just in time, leap out of the car, reload the briefcase with brochures and materials and rush in to perform the next sales meeting... and so the day goes on. Or if the salesperson is part of an internal sales team, the drive will be to record the key content of the telephone discussion on the CRM system and then move on to the next call in order to achieve the quantity of activity required for success. But because of the relentless pressure to do more and more, there's no time allocated to stopping for a few moments to think and review.   And without the reviewing there's not going to be any learning, exactly the situation that's illustrated in figure 3.

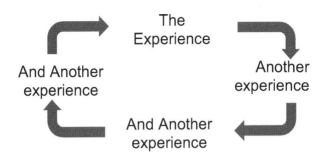

figure 3. The "No Learn" Cycle

> **Key thought: How many of your sales team are in the 'no learn cycle' every day rather than the learning cycle?**

Cramming as much as possible into every working day may contribute to achieving a high *quantity* of activity being Inputted into the job. But what about the learning, and so the *quality* of these Inputs? Unless time is invested to pause, review, think, and learn, the likelihood is that the salesperson will simply have the same experience, over and over again with no learning taking place along the way, no evolution in what they do and how they do these things, and so no increase in sales success. This is equally true for field based sales activity and telephone based sales activity. It's also potentially true of busy Sales Managers of course!

> **Key thought: How often do <u>you</u> proactively schedule time into the working day to reflect on what you're doing, how you're doing it, and what is and is not working most effectively - in order that <u>you</u> can continually improve the quality of <u>your</u> Inputs?**

And the irony for both face-to-face and telephone based selling situations is that the very time that there is the *most* need to learn and improve quality of the Inputs, there is probably going to be the strongest drive not to do it! This is what normally happens when salespeople fall behind target. Due to the task focused nature of the person in the role and their drive to achieve, the attitude kicks in that "...*I haven't got time to stop and think – I need to sell harder to make up the shortfall*". Even more troubling is that Sales Managers have a tendency to do exactly the same thing. When falling behind target, or during difficult economic periods and recessions, the mantra all too often becomes 'increase our sales activities'. Surely the mantra should become 'increase <u>the effectiveness</u> of our sales activities'.

> **Key thought: There's a big difference between 5 years' experience and one years' experience 5 times over! The former is achieved by constantly learning. A key responsibility of the Sales Manager is to make sure this happens.**

A critical part of the Sales Manager's role is to help the salesperson grow by maximising learning from their experiences. All of them. Or perhaps a more accurate way of saying the same thing, is that a critical challenge of the Sales Manager role is to interrupt the 'no learn cycle', and to provoke the salesperson to think in order that they can review, learn, and grow. Indeed, the Sales Manager has a responsibility to ensure growth is maximised from *all* potential learning situations, just some of which are listed in Table 1.

In terms of the *how to do this*, there are two critical skills and abilities that need to be called on. The first of these is coaching, which is of such importance and significance that the whole of chapter 3. of this book is devoted to it. The second is time management and organisation; unless the Sales Management activities which challenge the team to move out of the 'no learn cycle' and which help & support them to review experiences are prioritised, they are not going to happen. If the Sales Manager doesn't decide what the priorities of the Sales Manager role really are, there are always plenty of other people who will be happy to decide for them!

Day-to-day work
Presenting at sales meetings
Chairing / facilitating meetings
Formal training courses (internal and external)
e-learning
Internet based resources (reading, etc.)
Seminars & conferences
Books
Industry Journals and other publications
Shadowing / observing colleagues
Networking events

Table 1. Just some of the myriad of learning opportunities available today

Skills, Knowledge and Attitude

The three core components that underpin success in any and every job role, are knowledge, skills, and attitude. To successfully develop the sales team, it's important that the Sales Manager understands the difference between these three things, how each

19

contributes to success, and how they operate synergistically in order to make success happen.

Let's first of all differentiate between knowledge and skills… Knowledge is information and facts; a skill is the ability to actually do something. They are different, and to illustrate this, imagine for a moment someone who's learning how to swim. This individual might be able to describe how to dive into a swimming pool and move from one end of it to the other using a particular swimming stroke as the methodology – that's knowledge. Being able to actually do this is something different – that's a skill.

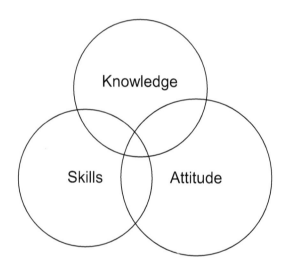

figure 4. The relationship between Skills, Knowledge and Attitude

A salesperson may well be able to describe the key elements that govern the structure for a successful face-to-face sales discussion or a proactive outbound telephone call; this does not though mean that they can do them. Knowing the structure is knowledge, being able to implement the structure successfully in the real world is a skill.

'Attitude' is a broad term that encompasses a package which includes confidence, self-belief, mind-set and values. The circle in figure 4. that represents 'attitude' is larger than the other two, as it's arguably the most important of the three components. Someone with high levels of skills & knowledge but low levels of confidence & self-belief and a cynical attitude to the role, is likely to struggle. An inexperienced person who has high energy and is bursting with enthusiasm and confidence is likely to succeed – though clearly, developing their skills & knowledge will sustain and enhance their success in the longer term.

Another way to think about this is to question which of the above two scenarios is easiest for the Sales Manager to 'fix'. I'd argue strongly that it's a lot easier to fix a lack of knowledge and/or skills than it is to 'fix' a lack of good attitude.

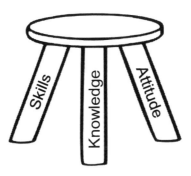

figure 5. The three components of Skills, Knowledge and Attitude can be thought of like the three legs of a three-legged stool…

Another way of considering the three components of knowledge, skills, and attitude is to think of them as being a little like the three legs of a three-legged stool (with the 'attitude' leg being a little more substantial than the other two). If any one leg of the stool is weak, not strongly linked with the other two, or even missing altogether, then things are likely to become rather wobbly! So for Sales Managers who are looking to maximise returns from investment in training & development, the message needs to be: Ensure that you've understood which of the three legs requires strengthening, and when growing the team in the longer term, do try to ensure that there's an equal focus on each of them.

> **Key thought: Considering each person in your team, how well developed are their skills, their levels of knowledge, and their attitude? Are they all balanced and working in synergy?**

Thinking back again to my time as a field based Sales Manager, there was one particular occasion which illustrates well the importance of mind-set and confidence…

Without going into the detail behind the story, the company I worked for at that time developed a special deal for a specific segment of the market. The customers in this particular segment regarded consistency of offer from suppliers to be a key issue. Unfortunately though, the company I worked for 'enjoyed' a reputation as being very **in**consistent (and the reputation was not without substance!) The deal that was on offer was competitive, and theoretically one that should have been perceived as attractive. As far as the customers were concerned though, because of our track record, the deal proved to actually be not very attractive at all.

As Regional Sales Manager, it was my responsibility to introduce the new deal to my sales team during one of our routine Regional meetings, and to ensure the team were well briefed, motivated, and fired up ready to exceed expectations. At that time the sales team I managed consisted of as wide a range of experience as you can imagine... from at one end of the spectrum graduates who were in their first ever job, through to highly experienced, high quality, and consistently successful, high performing, mature salespeople.

The reaction of the experienced in the team was predictable: they were frustrated by the inconsistent approach the company had taken over the years, and understood the damage this had inflicted on the company's brand. However, they were willing to 'give it their best'. And they did. But none of them quite achieved the sales objectives that had been set for the campaign.

One of the graduates in the team (a rookie), wasn't able to attend the sales meeting where the new deal had been briefed in (due to illness). So he received all the information about the deal 'at distance'. There was one piece of information that the briefing notes didn't provide him though... they didn't provide him an understanding of the history of the relationship between the company and the customer niche the deal was targeted at. Because of this he had no idea that there were likely to be some emotional barriers (from the customer's point of view) that would impact on success. The understanding *he* gained from the briefing notes, was that the deal was highly competitive, and that the customers targeted would feel the same. In short, we forgot to tell him that selling the deal was going to be difficult.

So this was a classic example of someone who as a rookie had limited knowledge and skills. But what he did have was a massive amount of enthusiasm (which was one of the reasons I'd hired him) and (admittedly because of a degree of naivety) a massive amount of confidence and high expectations of success.

The rest as they say is history. There was only one person in the Region who achieved their target for this deal – the salesperson who lacked knowledge and skills, but had a massive quantity of great attitude. The members of the team who enjoyed a massive quantity of knowledge and skills failed to achieve their sales objectives. And this was not because they had 'bad' attitude… in fact far from it. It was just that they didn't have the very positive mind-set their inexperienced colleague had.

Knowing what I do now, and with hindsight being the very exact science it is, what I really should have done was to work on the mind-set of the more experienced in the team. Clearly, the objectives we had been set were realistic – the inexperienced member of the team proved this to be the case. It's just that deep down, the more experienced in the team didn't *believe* the objectives were realistic. And that impacted on results.

> **Key thought: Henry Ford is quoted as saying "*Whether you think you can or think you can't – you're right*".**

The key issue: When focusing on training and developing the sales team, the Sales Manager does indeed need to ensure the required knowledge is provided, and does indeed need to help them acquire appropriate skills. Critical to success though is focusing on building 'attitude', and in particular, self-belief and confidence.

A training course may not be the answer…

In the past, if there was a need to enhance the knowledge and/or skills of an individual salesperson, or indeed of the sales team as a whole, then the solution was pretty well automatically to send them on a training course. That's one of the reasons why 'a development requirement' has become synonymous with 'a requirement to attend a training course'. This is not right though, as the requirement is not to attend a training course, it's to acquire specific knowledge and/or skills.

Today we have more options and alternatives in terms of ways to build skills and knowledge than ever before (see chapter 5.) An approach that suits one person doesn't necessarily suit another, and vice-versa – so the Sales Manager can take these individual preferences into account when choosing how each salesperson in the team is going to be developed. Cost-effectiveness is important too; why choose to implement a face-to-face training course for a field based sales team, for example (with all the associated costs of travel and accommodation), if a series of interactive webinars will achieve the development objectives?

Fact: It's estimated that around $15bn is spent on sales training annually – by US businesses alone(5).

Even more fundamental is the question: "*Is 'training' required at all?*" You may or may not have come across the story of the car mechanic who tended to forget to complete one part of a car service. So his employer sent him on a training course (an expensive option). It cured the problem. But then he began to forget to complete another and different part of the car service – so he was sent on another training course. And this proved to be just a temporary fix too, as not too long afterwards he began to forget to complete the part of the car service he was missing in the first place! Instead of sending him on an expensive training course surely it would have been easier – and a lot more effective - if he'd simply been provided with a small, laminated aid-memoire which listed all the items of the car service so he'd always have a reminder on him?! This would have been a rather less costly solution too. It comes back to what was mentioned above: The development need is for the garage mechanic to have the ability to remember all aspects of the car service that need to be carried out; the need <u>is not</u> to send him on a training course.

> **Key thought: When a salesperson has a development need, this does not automatically mean that they need to be sent on a training course.**

Once the (true) development need has been identified, the next questions are:
"*What different ways can this need be addressed?*"
"*What are the pros and cons of these approaches?*"
"*Which would work best?*"
"*…and most cost-effectively?*"

The point is, that the solution is not always a training course, and indeed not always training of any description. So when a sales team is failing to deliver against expectations the automatic answer should never be: "...*they need more training*" (which unfortunately can all too often be the knee-jerk reaction). Rather, the first step should always to be ascertain <u>why</u> they are *failing to deliver*. Once that critical question has been answered, and answered in full (as there might be a number of reasons, not just one), *then* appropriate solutions can be considered.

There's a rather inelegant question that I sometimes ask when meeting new clients for the first time and discussing what's perceived to be a training need in the sales team. This 'need' could be a failure to communicate effectively the value proposition, or to ask the customer for a commitment, or to pursue new prospects as well as manage established customer relationships. "*Imagine*", I say, "*that I was working with one of the team, and that I had a gun with me – and that I'd use it if they didn't do it*" (whatever 'it' is that they are not doing). "*Would they then do it?*" Quite often the answer to this question is: "*Yes – of course they would!*". In which case, the question – as inelegant as it is – has clarified a critical point: **There is no training need**. The salesperson already has the skills and know-how required – the skills and know-how are already 'in there' somewhere. The issue is, that the skills and knowledge that are already there are not being utilised effectively or not being used at all.

The salesperson knowing that I'm observing, and that there will be severe consequences if they don't do 'it' has changed the environment that the salesperson is operating in. And as a consequence of changing the environment the salesperson is now able to perform that task. No training has been provided, and so no new or extra skills or knowledge had been imparted. The underlying issue is not a training need... it's a *motivation* need.

> **Key thought: Be clear on what's causing the under-performance... a lack of skill, or a lack of will?**

Now clearly, when this question is asked, it needs to be asked with a great deal of tact and diplomacy! It does though make an important point. It doesn't necessarily mean that a workshop or event of some description is not an appropriate solution. It might be. But it most definitely *does* mean that the focus is not going to be on providing skills, knowledge and know-how, as those things are already there (to a greater or lesser degree). It's going to be about helping those attending to utilise and apply these things.

Before even considering if an event of some description is going to be appropriate though, it's essential to understand why the already acquired skills, knowledge and know-how are not being utilised. It could be because...

...the wrong environment is in place. The term 'environment' embraces everything that influences the motivation, thinking, and mind-set of the salesperson, and includes things like incentive programmes & reward systems, culture, and management style.

Take for example a situation I was asked to help with, where the sales team was failing to establish relationships with new (potential) key accounts. The perceived solution was a training course on how to win new key accounts, and this was why I was asked to provide support. During the initial client meeting I asked questions to gain a full understanding of what was influencing this issue, and it soon became clear that it was the environment within the organisation that was the main cause of it. The sales team were rewarded by a salary plus commission. The easiest way to achieve sales (and so commission) was to 'farm' well established relationships; in fact pursuing new and difficult to win key accounts would take time away from this higher-return, easy-earning activity, and so reduce earnings. More-over, the reward package of this organisation was very generous, so the opportunity to win new (difficult to win) key accounts wasn't of great interest to the sales team anyway – they were quite happy with the level of reward they were receiving already!

Training in how to win new key accounts may well have provided this sales team with more skills, knowledge and know-how than they already had. The likelihood is though that the investment in this training would have been a waste of resource (both training budget and time). The requirement was to influence the environment so that the sales team *wanted* to win more new key accounts. That alone might have solved the problem. And if it didn't fully solve the problem, then it would certainly have created a fertile environment into which appropriate training could have been added.

Key thought: There's a difference between spending money on training and investing in training. The latter achieves a healthy and impressive Return on Investment; the former just buys a training course with little or no returns.

...there is a lack of confidence. This could be for one or more of a number of reasons such as a lack of knowledge regarding a new segment of the market and so customer type that's being targeted, or eroded self-confidence due to the recent loss of an account. And each of these examples might require a different solution. Knowledge of the different customer type might be enhanced by inviting a guest speaker of this customer type to attend a sales meeting and provide a presentation about their industry, the needs and wants of their role, etc. An erosion of self-confidence might be addressed by a combination of manager coaching plus direct help and support. The point is though, that the automatic answer is most definitely not 'a training course'. It might be. But until the reason behind the issue is understood, what the most effective solution is can't be understood either.

...the right opportunities are not there. For example, if the winning of new appointments with prospects has been outsourced, and either there is an insufficient quantity of appointments being provided to the sales team, or because the quality of the appointments being provided is less than adequate. Or both! This would certainly impact on quantity of sales being achieved, and is likely to also impact on motivation, which will have a *further* negative effect on results.

...the right tools are not there. For example, the selling of a high value asset (e.g. plant & machinery) may require financial support such as leasing to be one part of the total solution. If there is no access to a leasing solution, or to one with competitive rates of interest, then it would be difficult to successfully sell against better armed and/or more cost-effective competition. Or a more simple example could be a sales team responsible for technical sales, who need to provide potential customers with a demonstration, and whose demonstration equipment is sub-standard. And an even more simple example would be a lack of clarity regarding the Value Proposition for what is being sold.

Interestingly, with all of the above points, it's the Sales Manager who should be able to remove the barriers to success. And since their job purpose is *to achieve sales through others*, removing these barriers should be the Sales Manager's priority (and responsibility).

Developing the skills of the sales team: Benefits

There is clearly a lot more to consider when growing and developing the sales team than simply organising a training course. And the pressured Sales Manager, with so many activities already on their agenda might (rightly) pose the fundamental question: "*Why bother with all these issues?*". The answer is: "*Because there are massive benefits*"...

- The sales team is better able to sell more and/or more effectively – supporting the Sales Manager's ability to achieve their job purpose of *achieving sales through others*.

- Supporting personal development is known to have a positive impact on both motivation and engagement – which again, will impact positively on sales success.

- Higher levels of engagement have also been shown to lead to a reduction in employee turnover – so less time and money will be spent on Recruitment & Selection.

- Higher tenure employees will be more experienced, and so have the potential to be higher performers.

- As the levels of ability within the sales team rise, perceptions of what are 'normal' levels of ability and achievement will rise too, leading to a general raising of standards.

- A more 'able' sales team requires less direct intervention by the Sales Manager; so more time can be focused on coaching and providing the support which helps to drive exceptional levels of success.

* A Sales Manager who enjoys a reputation of growing salespeople will attract higher quality candidates during the Recruitment & Selection process. This is particularly true for Generation Y.

* Supporting the sales team develop is great fun! And seeing them achieve personal growth is incredibly satisfying.

Now all this does not mean to suggest that the Sales Manager should be a professional sales trainer. In the same way that the Sales Manager's job purpose is to *achieve sales through others*, some aspects of developing the sales team can be achieved *through others* too. The purpose of this book is to provide Sales Managers with the understanding and know-how so that they can manage the development of the sales team in the most appropriate way, and know both what to do and how to do these things when it is indeed their input and activity that's required.

Summary

This chapter describes the key considerations which should be in the Sales Manager's mind when focusing on the activities which support the focus of this book: *Developing the skills of the sales team*.

A Sales Manager can be a great motivator, coach, and developer of people; what such a talented individual is able to achieve though will be limited by the quality of the people they have employed; you can't make a Stradivarius out a piece of old chipboard. And even having hired the right quality people, the expectations of the 'right material' from one generation might be different to another – and these different expectations need to be taken into account when supporting their personal development.

It's important to understand how people learn, which is by reviewing experiences. This in turn means that they need to have had an experience in the first place, and need to be helped and supported when reviewing these experiences. Chapter 3. which focuses on coaching considers how to do this in some depth.

Skills and knowledge are not the same; the latter is information, the former is the ability to perform a given action to recognised standards. Training can help to provide both of these things. The intangible issue of 'attitude' though is critical to success, and in particular the confidence and self-belief which drive and underpin 'attitude'. As Henry Ford stated: "*Whether you think you can, or think you can't, you're right*". Developing and growing the sales team therefore needs to include consideration of how to grow confidence and self-belief.

The good news for Sales Managers is that there are more options and alternatives in terms of *how* to provide training than ever before. This means that the most appropriate solution may not be a traditional training course – although there again it might! The key issue is to think through the pros and cons of the options available in order to identify which of these options is most appropriate.

However, before assuming that the answer is a training solution of any description, it's essential to understand what the underlying cause of the issue is in the first place: is it due to a lack of skill and/or knowledge, or is it due to a lack of confidence, or is it even possibly due to factors other than the salesperson? If so, then it might be that the most effective and appropriate solution isn't training at all.

2. Identifying Development Needs

I can remember even now what used to happen when I was a Sales Manager back in the 1980's, and the company I was working for conducted the annual Training Needs Analysis (TNA)... The training function offered a set of standard courses, some of which were provided via our own sales training team, and some of which were provided by external consultancies, and these were listed along with a description of what they were about in a comb-bound 'training course catalogue'. The idea was, that in conjunction with their line manager, each salesperson reviewed the courses listed in the brochure and chose to attend the course(s) that were appropriate for them - provided of course that their Sales Manager agreed with them. Not surprisingly, it was the training courses with the most interesting titles, and the ones with the most interesting content that were the most popular.

We're now 30+ years on from the 1980's, and there are still too many organisations that are taking this approach – which is wrong, and it's wrong for a number of reasons...

Firstly, this approach 'trains' the sales team (including Sales Management) to focus on courses, when what really should be focused on is the development need that the course helps to satisfy. It's not unlike when salespeople tell the customer all about what products and/or services they are selling without having found out first what the customer's needs and requirements are. Realistically, Sales Managers aren't necessarily provided with training which provides the know-how so they understand the importance of adopting a development need focused approach. As a consequence, the courses selected may well satisfy the emotional needs of the salesperson and their Sales Manager, but this does not necessarily mean that they are appropriate for the needs of the business.

Even worse, if selection of a course has not been driven by a clear understanding of what the gaps in skills and/or knowledge are, then it's impossible to assess whether the course has or has not plugged those gaps, which should be the measure of whether the training input has been successful or not. As a consequence, the way that 'effectiveness' of the course tends to be measured is by how much the participant thinks the course has helped – their perceptions. And perceptions tend to be influenced by how much the participant enjoyed the experience. And how much they enjoyed it can depend on how much fun they had during the course and the subject matter – which in turn can mean that an interesting course with an enticing title is attended, the Sales Manager subsequently receives positive feedback, and so recommends it to others in the team – be that course relevant to the development needs of the team or not!

> **Key thought: A Training Needs Analysis (TNA) is not a list of courses.**

A better approach to take is to firstly clarify exactly what the skill and/or knowledge gaps are. This might be a lack of skills and/or knowledge to achieve in the role as it is today, or a requirement to acquire new skills and/or knowledge in advance of an anticipated evolution in the market place or in advance of a move to a different role in the business. Or indeed a change in focus of the sales role, towards more key account activity, for example. Once that the true development need has been understood, then the most appropriate way of providing the skills, knowledge and know-how that are required can be considered.

Approaching a TNA in this way also begins to provoke thought about what 'success' will look like, 'success' being a healthy return on the investment (ROI) of the time and resource that's required. If there's an understanding of what the participant wants to be able to do differently as a consequence of the development activity, then this can be measured (more discussion on the objective measurement of ROI in chapter 4.)

Effectiveness of training will also be enhanced, as those attending understand that they are not there with the goal of attending a training course and being there for the day, or two days, or whatever the duration of the course is - but to develop specific skills and know-how for use in their role after the event. There is clarity that the activity is a meaningful one, and that there are clear expectations in terms of application of learning afterwards.

This doesn't suggest that a company should not have a set of standard development events that provide core skills and know-how. Indeed, if a company has identified precisely what knowledge and skills a salesperson needs to acquire when they first join the company, and also need adding to in order to develop more advanced skills, then it makes good sense to design high quality training which provides them. This is what a robust sales academy structure should do.

It's the philosophy though of asking first of all "*What do you want to do differently / better?*" then identifying the gaps in skills, and/or knowledge, and then identifying how best to provide what's missing, that's important.

One way of approaching this is to conduct a TNA using something like the form illustrated in figure 6.

Skill area	Relevance to current role					Assessment of ability				
Structuring the sales discussion	1	2	3	4	5	1	2	3	4	5
Effective questioning skills	1	2	3	4	5	1	2	3	4	5
Listening skills	1	2	3	4	5	1	2	3	4	5
Communicating competitive advantage	1	2	3	4	5	1	2	3	4	5
Presenting benefits	1	2	3	4	5	1	2	3	4	5
Persuasiveness	1	2	3	4	5	1	2	3	4	5
Adapting style to different personality types	1	2	3	4	5	1	2	3	4	5
Managing customer concerns	1	2	3	4	5	1	2	3	4	5
Gaining the commitment	1	2	3	4	5	1	2	3	4	5

Figure 6. A questionnaire that can be used to provoke thought about training needs

Asking each member of the sales team to complete this can be an effective way of provoking thought about what their development needs really are, and how important it is to address them. It might be that a given salesperson perceives themselves to have a relatively low level of a particular skill, but that it also contributes little to achieving in the role. So whilst there is a skills gap, it's not necessarily a development priority.

A constructive way of using this tool is for each salesperson in the team and their Sales Manager to complete this independently (by simply circling or highlighting the appropriate number). Comparing the two sets of perceptions during a one-to-one 'meeting of minds' can form the basis of useful, productive, and positive discussion. At the very least, we know that the Sales Manager demonstrating that they have a genuine enthusiasm to support the salesperson to develop and grow will have a positive impact on levels of engagement[6], which in turn is categorically linked to higher performance[7].

> **Key thought: A Training Needs Analysis is about identifying the gaps in skills and knowledge that are required to succeed in the role.**

The problem with taking an approach like this though is that it's subjective, so based purely on opinion regarding both levels of ability and relevance to the job. My own experience has shown that ironically it's normally the most talented and successful salespeople in the team who are the most self-critical, and so often rate their abilities lower than the less talented members of the team do. Perhaps that's a trait of the more successful... that they are more self-critical and constantly seek ways to improve their skills so they can improve the quality of what they do. I've also noted that the less successful are more comfortable and satisfied with their levels of skills, and their perceptions of their skill levels don't necessarily match with what I observe when accompanying them when they're doing the job. One of the reasons for the Sales Manager to also conduct the analysis therefore is to help overcome any misconceptions. Indeed, for the more successful who tend to be quite self-critical, receiving feedback that the Sales Manager's perceptions (and the opinion a professional and respected observer) of their skills and abilities is higher than their own, can actually be quite motivational.

The more that TNA's can be driven by an **objective** assessment of gaps in skills and knowledge though, the better...

Knowing what to focus on: Sales Process

A Sales Process is a recognised set of repeatable actions, which when implemented in a specific order and to a defined quality, will achieve the same outcome – or at least are more likely to. Because selling involves the vagaries of people and emotions, and because each selling scenario will be different, the outcome can never be an absolute certainty. It *is* true though, that if the right Sales Process is implemented consistently and to the required quality, the desired result (which of course is sales) is certainly a lot more likely to happen consistently also. So for Sales Managers, the challenge is to *ensure* it's being implemented consistently and to the required quality.

The sales process illustrated in figure 7. is clearly a very simple example, and most sales processes will be more complex than this. None-the-less, it illustrates well an important point, and that is that once the sales process has been defined, the success rate at each step in the process can be measured. This data can be utilised to identify where the sales process is being executed efficiently, and points in the process where selling efficiency can be improved. For example, for the simple sales process illustrated in figure 7., it would be useful to measure the proportion of follow-up appointments which lead to achievement of the desired commitment ('sign-up'), and the success rate when making appointment-winning telephone calls. These are conversion ratios, and comparing the conversion ratios of different members of the team can be used to identify who is particularly successful at a given step, and indeed who is not. For those who are less successful, it may well mean that there is an opportunity to improve their performance - they have a development need.

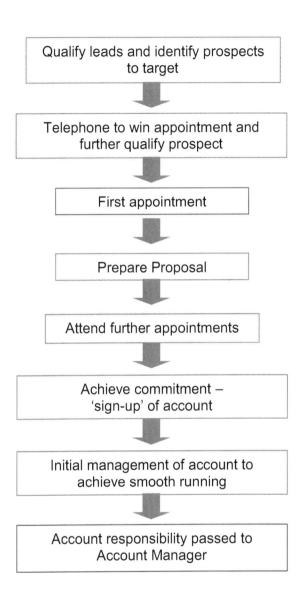

figure 7. A simple Sales Process

Key thought: Understanding conversion ratios can help to identify development needs

---

Note here that the term is 'development need', and not necessarily 'training need'. It could be that coaching, mentoring, or the Sales Manager helping to bolster confidence would provide the development that's required, and that a 'formal' training course is not the most appropriate answer. A training course could be the most appropriate answer though.

By looking at the objective data (the conversion ratios), the Sales Manager has identified a specific development need and can now consider the most appropriate way to address this need. Adopting this sort of approach is a lot more targeted, professional, and efficient than simply putting the salesperson on to a standard 'sales training' course because their overall sales figures aren't quite what they need to be.

This approach to identifying development requirements can be made specific to the individual salesperson too; there's no point in all the sales team attending a workshop focused on the acquisition of specific skills and know-how if some in the team already have them and are applying them successfully. Having said that, there are some circumstances where attendance of an event by already skilled members of the team might be desirable. For example, if one of the goals of a workshop is teambuilding, and the reason that the more successful and already skilled are there is to pass on their expertise & know-how, and *not* having the team together as one Group is something that the Sales Manager wants to avoid. If the reason to bring the team together can be justified, then that's fine. Understanding individual salesperson conversion ratios provides the Sales Manager with the information and data required to underpin an objective decision making process.

It might also be though that *everyone* in the sales team is achieving a lower conversion ratio at one or more points in the sales process than might be expected. The first question that needs to be asked in these situations of course is "*Why?*" If it is due to a lack of skills and/or knowledge, then there is indeed a training need for the sales team as a whole, and then the Sales Manager can consider the best way of addressing this team development requirement.

And of course if this team requirement turns out to be an issue for the entire sales team nationally, or indeed globally, then addressing this development requirement becomes a company-wide issue.

The world continues to evolve…

The challenges of all customers of all industries continue to change, and so too therefore do the needs and requirements that they want their suppliers and partners to address. Sales professionals need to understand their customers, be able to empathise with their issues and problems, provide appropriate solutions to these issues and problems, and be able to use compelling arguments to effectively sell these solutions. And of course they need to have the confidence to do this. Providing appropriate training to ensure the sales team retain an up to date awareness and understanding of the customer's environment in order that they can do this is important.

Even more important though is providing insight into *expected and potential* changes in the customer's environment in order that the sales team can in turn provide insight to their customers. It's far better to be positioned in the competitive market places we operate in today as helping customers remain ahead of any changes to their world, rather than helping them to react to these changes after they've happened. Moreover, it this is done before and/or better than is done by your competition, this will help to develop competitive advantage. The proposition is no longer just the product and/or the service that's being sold; part of the proposition becomes the insight the sales team provides – a difference that's not necessarily easy to emulate.

> **Key thought: What is being done currently to provide your sales team with an understanding of how the world of your customers is expected to evolve? And how to utilise this information in order to enhance relationships, better differentiate from the competition, and so win more sales?**

Training & development for the sales team also needs to be sensitive to the fact that the way organisations purchase is continually evolving. It's certainly true that the global economic challenges of 2007 and 2008 accelerated change. Purchasing cycles are longer, salespeople today access the purchasing cycle later, and when they do, the customer is more educated about both the needs they have and the potential solutions that can help them manage these needs. Customer expectations of suppliers and the skill levels of suppliers sales teams are certainly higher. The role of Procurement is changing too; in many organisations Procurement have a more strategic role than they used to, wield more power, and are involved earlier in the purchasing process.

In short, the way that organisations buy today is different, which logically means that the sales training that professional sales people are provided needs to be different too. Providing exactly the same sales training that was provided a few years ago simply doesn't make any logical sense. Which begs the question of course about the sales training that your organisation is providing… how well has it evolved and adapted in tandem with the evolution we've seen over the last few years? And if using an external sales training consultancy then the same question applies to what they are providing.

For Sales Managers, all this means two things:

1) There is a need to understand how the way that customers purchase has evolved, and to provide appropriate support so that the sales team can evolve their approach in tandem with this, and..

2) …there is a need to understand how the challenges of the customer are going to evolve in the future – and to arm the sales team in advance with the skills, knowledge and know-how which will enable them to help the customer proactively manage these challenges.

Keeping up with leading thinking

It's important to retain an up-to-date awareness and understanding of 'state of the art' knowledge related to professional sales. For Sales Managers who enjoy the resources of an internal sales training specialist, then this really should be part of their remit. However, at the end of the day it's the Sales Manager who is reliant on the sales team having cutting edge skills, knowledge and abilities, so it should be the Sales

Manager who should *want* to retain an up-to-date understanding of trends and thinking. After all, it would be quite strange if Sales Managers *were not* interested in what the more forward thinking and effective sales organisations were doing! Such an up-to-date understanding can be easily achieved via membership of professional sales institutes, and by attending relevant conferences and seminars. It's important to ensure though that seminars attended have a robust content - too many are simply 'motivational' ("Ra Ra"!) meetings where the content is rather shallow and based on subjective opinion rather than facts. Attendance of the more robust seminars and conferences will enable the Sales Manager to retain an awareness of relevant research, what the more successful organisations are doing, etc.

Key thought: In the UK the Sales Performance Association provides 4 seminars annually, for more details see www.salesperformanceassociation.com

I visited a UK based organisation a while back to learn about what they had done to achieve the accolade "European Call Centre of the Year", and indeed what they were continuing to do in order to retain the impressively high standards they'd achieved. I was fascinated to learn about how they proactively engaged with other organisations so they could learn about what these organisations were doing and the ideas they were implementing successfully. There was actually a senior manager whose full time role was doing only this! This organisation is a very large national company and a 'house hold' name. They reach out to similarly large national 'house hold' names, their offer being to share the good practice that they've developed in return for the other organisations doing the same – networking at a corporate level!

There is no reason why the Sales Manager can't adopt a similar approach when networking at external meetings, seminars and conferences…

There is also the opportunity to compare the abilities of the team against what's been identified as the skill and knowledge requirements for that particular sales role. National Occupational Standards can be helpful here, and there's more discussion about what these are and how to use them in chapter 8.

180 degree and 360 degree feedback

180 and 360 degree feedback are means of gaining feedback from others regarding their perceptions. '360 degree' feedback is the term that's used when those who provide the feedback are at all 'levels' around you – so senior to you, at peer level, those who report to you – hence the term '360 degree'. 180 degree feedback is when those who provide feedback are all peers at the same 'level' as you in the organisation. Feedback can be acquired on any aspect of performance, and so help to identify development needs.

Both 180 and 360 degree feedback normally involves use of some sort of on-line questionnaire. Those who are going to be providing the feedback are first of all invited to participate, and they in due course go on-line to complete the questionnaire. Feedback provided needs to be both honest and accurate, so it's important to ensure that those providing feedback know the person well and want to support the process. What's to be avoided is a situation where, for example, a customer or colleague chooses the option 'unobserved', and so provides no useful information. Or even worse provides negative feedback which is based on inaccurate assumptions because they simply don't know the person very well.

Once everyone has provided feedback, their input is collated in a report and used to inform a discussion between the individual concerned and an appropriately trained coach. This conversation recognises areas of strength, and also identifies areas where the perceptions of those who provided feedback suggests there may be a development need. Very frequently, the person who's receiving the feedback will also have completed the same questionnaire, in order that they can compare their own perceptions with the perceptions of others.

figure 8. A 360 degree feedback tool
(by kind permission of The Communication
Challenge Limited. All rights reserved.)

With such feedback tools, it's not the actual questionnaire and data that are of most importance – it's the coaching conversation that's driven by the data that's of most importance. And of course the most important outcome of this conversation is the development of an **Action Plan** to address agreed development needs, and then its subsequent implementation. *How well* the process has addressed the development needs can be measured by repeating the same exercise again after an appropriate period of time, and seeing if the perceptions of others have changed as a consequence of Action Plan implementation.

For these tools to be effective, it's essential that 1) those providing input are open, honest, candid, and feel comfortable participating, and 2) those who are receiving the feedback are open and responsive to it. Both these things are influenced by the culture of the organisation. The tools work very effectively in organisations where such a positive, open, and vibrant culture exists.

Where the culture is not one that supports their use, then they need to be used with great caution, or not even at all. For example, if the individual receiving the feedback feels threatened, or perceives that negative feedback from others will be damaging to their career progression, then the exercise is likely to damage morale and motivation rather than enhance these things. This is not supportive of the Sales Manager's goal of achieving sales through others; so at fear of stating the obvious it would not be a good idea to go ahead!

If the culture within the organisation is not conducive to the use of these tools, but there is a desire to evolve the culture to one which is more supportive of their use, then the recommended way forward is to initially implement something very simple and nonthreatening within the team, and then slowly over a period of time move to a deeper and more meaningful approach. There's also the opportunity for the Sales Manager to act as a role model, and to use this approach to support their own personal development. Again, this requires the sales team to feel comfortable about providing honest and accurate feedback, and that whatever feedback is provided will not result in any negative consequences to them! Most on-line tools provide anonymity, so when the results are being reviewed all that's known is the number of respondents who've provided which response to each question. If the sales team as a whole feel that the Sales Manager will react badly to feedback other than that which is positive, then there's still likely to be a fear that it will be possible to discern precisely what feedback each individual salesperson has given via a little logic and detective work! Mind you, if this is the feeling of the sales team, then the behaviours of the Sales Manager need to change in order to develop a more open culture. 'Command and Control' cultures are not appropriate today, and pragmatically, we know that more open cultures are associated with more productive and profitable organisations. They're much nicer places to be too.

If there is a desire to use feedback tools of this type, and they have not been used before, then it's strongly advised that the wise counsel of an appropriately qualified and experienced person is sought. The most appropriate person will be a colleague in HR. There is the option of gaining input and guidance from an external consultancy who provides these tools, and with the enormous amount of experience they will have of using these tools in all sorts of different companies and circumstances, then this is certainly an option that's worth considering. The one caveat is the obvious one, which is that they have something to gain by providing the potential purchaser with confidence that the tool can be used successfully. So an independent source of advice is arguably more appropriate. And if there isn't an internal HR resource, other options available include external HR consultancy support, or even advice via on-line forums such as those on LinkedIn.

The business culture of the geographical Region will also influence how feasible it is to utilise these instruments. Both France and Germany have a business culture where the use of feedback instruments is difficult due to the influence of works councils and other employee representative bodies. In the Asia Pacific Region, to question or provide negative feedback to someone within an organisation who is 'senior' and so 'above you' in the hierarchy, is totally in contradiction with the culture there.

360 feedback: Example data

Take a look at figure 9. This shows what just one page of data could look like for a salesperson who's using a 360 degree feedback tool to inform a coaching conversation. The on-line questions will have been responded to by their immediate line manager, their colleagues, a selection of their customers, and the salesperson themselves. This particular page is just one of a much larger report, and provides a summary of how customers have responded to a number of questions, and how this compares to the response that the salesperson has given.

(The vertical line '0' in the centre represents the average score of all respondents; so any bar to the left means 'below average', and any to the right 'above average)

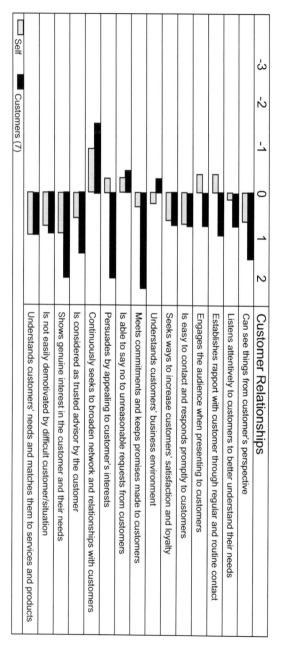

figure 9. Possible feedback – customer
(by kind permission of The Communication Challenge Limited. All rights reserved.)

There is an enormous amount of data here on just one page. The person who is to coach the salesperson would review this in advance of meeting with them for their debrief, and have identified all the key points which need to be discussed during the coaching conversation. From just this one page the points to highlight are:

- Both the salesperson and customers rate 'Can see things from the customer's perspective' as above average. This is an opportunity to positively reinforce what is clearly already being done quite well.

- There is more good news related to 'Meets commitments and keeps promises made to customers'. Whilst the salesperson perceives that they do deliver in this area, the customer has an even stronger perception related to this than they do! So the message for the salesperson to take away from a coaching conversation would be: "*Yes, it's good to be striving to improve how you meet commitments and keep promises. But right now, your customers have positive perceptions of you here. Well done!*"

- Both the salesperson and customers rate 'Continuously seeks to broaden network and relationships with customers' as significantly below average. This is an area which therefore requires some attention, and so agreement of what's going to happen to address this shortfall – the **Action Plan**. If the salesperson doesn't know how to 'broaden network and relationships with customers', then there is a training need.

- Both the salesperson and customers rate performance against the two points 'Is considered as trusted advisor by the customer' and 'Shows genuine interest in the customer

53

and their needs' as above average. And similar to above, customers have an even more positive perception than the salesperson does.

These are just some of the highlights from just one page of what would be a substantial report. It would be interesting, for example, to see what the perceptions of this individual's manager and their colleagues were against issues such as 'Meets commitments and keeps promises made to customers'. The person who provides feedback and reviews this data, needs to be a properly trained and qualified coach; a huge amount of data is acquired from both 180 and 360 degree feedback instruments and it's important that this data is understood fully, and utilised in the right way, to inform a motivational coaching conversation which drives the development of an Action Plan which enhances the ability of the salesperson to utilise higher quality Inputs. Which will of course drive a higher quality and/or quantity of Outputs.

Build on strengths…

When considering development needs, there's traditionally tended to be a focus on identifying areas where the individual is least talented and skilled, in order that they can be provided help to develop in this area and so to improve performance overall. But is this really the best approach and mind-set…?

Imagine for a moment Cristiano Ronaldo… Real Madrid's star striker, the only person to have won the 'European Golden Shoe' award four times, and reputed to be the world's best football player (and some would say the world's best football player *ever*). It would be absolute nonsense for his coach to say to him: "*Cristiano, you're an incredible striker, and one who puts fear into the hearts of the opposition. But you really aren't that good playing midfield, and certainly lack skills as a defender. So we're going to put together a training programme which will help you in these areas...*"

Or for Lewis Hamilton's coach to say to him: "*Lewis, no British driver has won the F1 championship more times than you. That's a fantastic achievement, and you are clearly at the top of your game. But you really could be a bit better at racing motor bikes. So we're going to put together a training programme which will help you with this...*"

Or Adam Vinatieri, the awesome placekicker of the Indianapolis Colts of the US National Football League (NFL), who holds several NFL records for his kicking, to be told by his coach: "*Great job Adam... but I can see an opportunity for us to improve your tackling, and we're going to put together a training programme which will help you with this...*"

Saying these things would, of course, be absolute nonsense! Why on earth would someone who's at the top of their game focus on something they're not good at?!

Using sports analogies to communicate messages to business professionals and in particular sales professionals can be a little dangerous; not everything applies in the same way in these different worlds. But it does provide some food for thought about a number of issues...

Key thought: It's tough getting to the top; it's arguably even harder staying there!

Firstly, every NFL player can't achieve excellence in every position on the playing field. People apply the core talents they have in order to excel at a particular team role. The same is true of soccer players. And just because someone is an extraordinary F1 racing car driver, it doesn't mean that they are going to be great at racing motorbikes. It's the same in professional sales. Just because someone is particularly talented at winning new business, it doesn't necessarily mean that they are going to excel at account management. For Sales Managers, this means that it's critical to help each member of the sales team understand what their core strengths are, and the role and environment which will allow them to excel. Never ask or encourage someone to be what they are not.

Secondly, sports professionals who've reached the top of their game practice, practice, practice. They avoid complacency and keep rehearsing for success by practicing what they are already good at. That's not a bad philosophy to encourage the experienced members of the team to embrace – keep practicing what you're already good at to *retain* excellence.

It's also true that the very top sports professionals don't know how to enhance performance without the assistance of video technology. F1 drivers review videos of the practice laps they have before the actual race in order to identify how to shave off every 0.1 of a second in time they can, on each of the corners of the racing track. Maybe a good way of helping the more successful in the team identify how to improve their performance would be to take a similar approach – with a day of video-recorded exercises that they can review with the support and assistance of a professional sales coach. Pilots, professional drivers and other professions have 'review courses' where they simply take time out to review how they are applying their skills, as a 'fail safe' check to ensure that the quality of what they do hasn't diminished at all. Maybe this is another philosophy the Sales Manager can encourage the top professionals in their team to embrace…

> **Key thought: Amateurs practice until they get it right; professionals practice until they can't get it wrong…**

Sports coaches also tend to coach positively, i.e. they focus the mind of the professional sportsperson on identifying what they are doing well and what's driving the achievement of results. This avoids inadvertently building up the subconscious mind set of '*I can't*', or '*this is going to be difficult for me*'. Sales Managers would do well to adopt an approach that develops and nurtures a mind-set that '*I can*'…

Realistically, it may be that a given individual in the sales team does have a significant development need… a significant gap in their skills set which the term 'weakness' might be an accurate description of. And of course these gaps need to be plugged if they are hampering achievement in the role, as that will in turn hamper the Sales Manager's ability to achieve sales through others. The critical point this short section is aiming to communicate though is about the Sales Manager's mind set when identifying training needs: by all means address weaknesses if they are there… but also recognise strengths. Tap into them, build on them, and help the salesperson to continue to excel at what they are already really good at. Sometimes that alone is challenging. And indeed sometimes that alone is enough.

Summary

When considering what development opportunities should be provided to the sales team, the fundamental question that needs to be asked first of all is: "*What are their development requirements?*".

Trying to answer this question by simply providing a list of courses is not the most appropriate way forward. To provide an analogy... in a consultative selling environment, the most ineffective selling approach is for the salesperson to simply provide the customer with a list of products and/or services and ask them to 'take their pick'. Businesses today want to partner with organisations whose salespeople ask questions in order to identify the needs and requirements that they have, and as a consequence to then be able to propose the most appropriate and cost-effective solution(s). Indeed, we know that the most effective salespeople are those who, as part of this process, ask the sort of questions which *help the customer* to think, and so to better understand the needs and requirements they have.

A robust TNA should be similar, and should be about identifying the development needs of the salesperson and the sales team as a whole. And if the TNA is conducted in a way which enables *the salesperson* to think and as a consequence better understand their areas of strength and the areas which require development, then so much the better. Only after the development needs have been fully understood is it possible to develop an Action Plan which will provide the support required, and provide it in the most appropriate way.

This isn't to say that a 'standard' suite of development events and courses is not appropriate. Quite the contrary. Providing standard events to address common development needs achieves continuity across the organisation, and as a bonus can help to achieve cost-savings (via economies of scale etc.). Beware though creating the environment where the most interesting course attracts the most participants because it's interesting, rather than because it's most appropriate to the needs of the business.

Simple subjective tools such as the one illustrated in figure 6. can be used to provoke thought, and be used to inform coaching style conversations and a 'meeting of minds' between the Sales Manager and individual salespeople within the team.

360 and 180 degree feedback tools can be helpful too. They certainly provide an immense amount of data. However, what's most important is not so much the data, but the coaching conversation that the data fuels. Culture influences whether these tools should be utilised or not – and this relates to both the culture of the business and the business culture of the country where the organisation operates.

The aforementioned tools focus on the abilities of the sales team today. The skills and know-how that make the professional salesperson successful today are not necessarily identical to those that are going to underpin future success. It's important therefore to consider how the role of the sales team is going to evolve in order to arm them with appropriate skills and know-how *in advance* of any changes that are going to be required. This could happen because of a change in focus by the selling organisation, and/or by a change in the environment that targeted customers operate in, which in turn changes what they purchase and/or how they purchase.

It's important to keep abreast of what the more successful sales organisations are doing, and the thoughts of leading thinkers in sales. Attendance of seminars and membership of relevant Institutes and other organisations will help with this.

Finally, be aware that everyone in the sales team will have strengths. It's all too easy to find fault and find what salespeople can't do as effectively as they could, or even not do at all. Sometimes a more effective approach is to understand what salespeople *can* do – their strengths – and to build on these things...

3. Coaching

Coaching is one of the most important skills for a Sales Manager to acquire and develop – if not *the* most important one. Sales Managers can use coaching skills to…

…help each salesperson grow their skills and know-how.

…bolster the levels of confidence each salesperson enjoys.

…build a culture of 'ownership' within the sales team.

…maximise ROI from all the team's development activities.

…help the sales team develop team solutions to team issues.

…drive higher levels of both motivation and engagement.

…provide superior briefings when delegating.

…reduce the amount of time the Sales Manager spends on tasks which should be done by the sales team.

…increase staff retention.

That's quite some list, particularly when it's considered that all of these outcomes help the Sales Manager to achieve their job purpose of *achieving sales through others*. If there was a product for sale in the market place which was proven to help achieve *just one* of these things, the chances are that it would be a best-seller! Coaching doesn't just help achieve one of them though, it helps to achieve <u>all</u> of them.

Unlike a product being sold on the market though, the key to opening the gateway to all of these benefits doesn't cost any money. It does require an investment of effort, and of course an initial investment for the

Sales Manager to learn what coaching is, and to develop the ability to be able to coach – so the acquisition of coaching skills. Once basic coaching skills are on board though, they are there for life. There's always the option to later on further fine tune, refine, and develop these skills, and there are many courses and other development events which can help with this.

Once coaching skills have been acquired, it's not unlike when you've acquired the skills required to ride a bicycle. Even if you've not ridden a bicycle for a long time, the moment you're back in the saddle again, isn't it remarkable how quickly and easily you automatically remember what you're supposed to do? OK, you might be a little wobbly to begin with, and you might (rightly) feel that your skills are a little rusty. They do soon return though. And that's what coaching is like too.

> **Key thought: You don't forget how to ride a bicycle. Coaching skills are a bit like that...**

In the same way that reading a book about the skills of swimming can't teach you how to swim, whilst this chapter provides a solid understanding of what coaching entails and how to coach, reading the chapter in isolation of practicing can't provide coaching *skills*. Like any skill, the only way to learn and develop coaching skills is to do it. This chapter provides sufficient information to enable Sales Managers to begin to apply the core principles of coaching with their team, and it's this 'doing' which will actually help to develop the skills. And referring back to the learning cycle again, it's the doing... followed by the reviewing of what worked well and could have been done better... which enables learning... and will inform planning about how to coach even better next time around.

For Sales Managers reading this book: if you've not already attended a course which at least includes within it a section on coaching skills, or even better attended one totally dedicated to this key subject, then I'd recommended that you do. This chapter hopefully will provide the inspiration for you to make this commitment!

Why coaching is important – the proof

In simple terms, all the benefits listed at the beginning of this chapter are descriptions of how coaching drives higher levels of skills, knowledge, and attitude. And these three things most certainly underpin sales success. But is there an unequivocal and proven link between Sales Managers who coach, coach more often, coach more effectively, and consequential sales success?

The short answer is a categorical **"Yes"**.

In 2000, the Business School of Cardiff University in the UK published the results of a survey focussed on B2B sales organisations(8). As the results are simply observations of what the successful and not so successful sales organisations do and do not do, and more importantly what the differences between them are, the comments and conclusions of the investigators are of high significance to organisations which aim to maximise returns from their sales resource.

Amongst what were referred to as "The Hallmarks of Effective Sales Organisations" the authors listed:

- Sales Managers spending less time selling and more time managing and coaching sales people.
- Higher levels of behaviour-based control by sales managers and higher quality performance of these activities.
- Superiority in salesperson performance driven by superiority in behavioural performance.

NB The term 'behaviour' means what a person does and/or what they say, so in relation to salespeople, these are their Inputs.

It's important to emphasise that the word 'control' does not necessarily mean 'tell', or 'direct'. Enabling the sales team to think things through by asking them questions – which is what coaching is all about – is a highly effective means of 'controlling' sales behaviours. In fact, since people take ownership of solutions when they've thought them through for themselves and come to a decision themselves about what the best thing to do is, coaching is arguably the most effective 'controlling' strategy the Sales Manager has.

So, to simplify the language of this quote from the survey, the authors have concluded that the more successful Sales Managers invest less time selling themselves, invest more time in coaching, are better at coaching, and that their sales teams as a consequence become more effective at selling, and as a consequence of that sell more. That's quite a compelling argument in favour of Sales Managers investing time to coach, and to conduct coaching to a high quality.

The authors further observed: "...*sales managers in the more effective sales units invest more of their effort in all aspects of behaviour control activities...*", and "*This has interesting implications for sales*

manager training and development".   For sales managers, all this provokes three important questions:
1) Am I allocating sufficient time to observing my team in the real world, and then coaching in order to improve their skills? and
2) Have I already invested sufficiently in my personal development in this area in order that I can coach effectively? and
3) What extra would the team achieve if I coached more effectively and more often?

Key thought: Want to emulate what the more successful Sales Managers in the more successful B2B sales organisations do? They invest more time coaching than the less successful, they are more highly skilled in this area, and so the coaching they conduct is of a higher quality.

A second thought-provoking study was conducted by Nationwide Building Society(9).   This financial institution offers a wide range of products to the consumer market place in the UK, including loans, mortgages and savings products.   To find out specifically what drives success and profitability, Nationwide provided (independent) statisticians based at the University of Bath with an enormous amount of data about the organisation, and challenged them to identify from this data specifically what it is that drives sales success.   Information from employee surveys, about their employees (tenure, backgrounds, etc.), about their branches (location, etc.) and of course detailed sales data, were all provided. Analysing this mass of data would be quite some task; finding statistically significant relationships between sales success and specific parts of the data though would clearly help to define what 'best practice' means, and so would help to guide recommendations regarding what should and should not be high priority activities and / or actions in the future.

This enormous piece of work identified (with very high statistical significance) five factors which drive sales success and profitability. One of these five is coaching of the branch staff by the branch manager. Not surprisingly, quality coaching by branch managers is considered to be a high priority activity – as it's been categorically shown to drive sales success.

The examples of objective studies that have demonstrated – emphatically and impressively – that effective coaching results in higher performance by sales teams goes on and on and on...

Dixon and Adamson reported in the Harvard Business Review that effective coaching achieved a sustained increase in sales performance of up to +19%[10]. And in the same journal, Hubbard reported a study which showed that in the finance sector when sales leaders invested more time coaching "...win rates of forecasted deals went up by 8.2 percent and the percentage of overall revenue attainment was 5.2 percent higher"[11].

There are plenty of good theoretical reasons to suspect that effective sales coaching increases the success of sales teams. Indeed, you'll hear plenty of anecdotal evidence from successful sales leaders regarding how their use of a coaching focused approach has had a *massive* impact on sales success. The link between coaching and sales success is not just theoretical and not just based on subjective opinion though – it's real, tangible, and has been measured objectively – time and time again. **Sales Managers who coach effectively, and**

consciously invest time to do this, are more successful.

And that's why an entire chapter of this book is devoted to just this one subject.

Coaching – what it is and what it isn't

In the context of the learning cycle discussed earlier, coaching is the skill of helping and supporting the salesperson to review, learn, and plan. It's a salesperson focussed activity which applies questioning and listening skills in order to provoke them to think for themselves, and to help them reach their own conclusions based on rational thought. The role of the coach during coaching is to remain impartial. It's most definitely not to tell the salesperson what to think and do – it's to help them to do the thinking and to work out the answers for themselves. In short, the role of the coach is not to 'put in', the role of the coach is to 'draw out'. So coaching does not involve providing opinion, telling, directing or persuading... coaching involves asking questions in order to help the coachee (i.e. the person who is being coached) to think things through for themselves.

> **Key thought: The role of the coach is not to 'put in', it's to 'draw out'.**

When coaching, the opinion of the coach is irrelevant, and so should not be provided or even hinted at all. The one aspect of persuasion that does come into coaching is from the point of view of the person being coached. A good coach enables the coachee to *persuade themselves* what the best way forward is based on an objective appraisal of the options that they have.

When first embracing this key skill, Sales Managers normally find coaching quite difficult and challenging. This isn't surprising though when you consider the sales background that they've come from. Selling is about being persuasive, providing information, and using influencing skills in order to bring the other party towards your way of thinking. Coaching is almost the very opposite of this. It's not about being persuasive, and it's not about trying to reach a pre-defined conclusion such as a commitment to purchase (although the pre-defined end-point in coaching is that there will be an agreed plan of some description). It is the coachee who arrives at the conclusion that's right for them, with the coach helping them along the journey that they travel on to this conclusion.

Coaching then is very different to providing direction, where the manager *tells* the salesperson specifically what to do and/or how to do it. Coaching is about helping the salesperson to work out for themselves the most appropriate thing(s) to do and how to do them.

Coaching is also different to giving feedback. Giving feedback (which will be explored in more depth later) is where the manager provides objective information in order to support learning. This might be part of the coaching process, but it is not actually coaching (more about this subtle differentiation later).

Coaching is also not training. Training is when skills and/or knowledge are provided. Training is about 'putting in'. Coaching is about 'drawing out' once skills and knowledge have been 'put in'. Take an example of a newly appointed and inexperienced salesperson who's participating in their first ever sales training course... if a (coaching) question was asked before they attended the course like "*So, in order to help us to plan and prepare for the meeting you have with [company name] on Thursday, remind me… what's the overall structure we know describes an effective sales meeting?*" the answer would probably be: "*Sorry – I've no idea!*". The problem is, that information hasn't yet been 'put in', and it's very difficult to draw something out if it isn't in there in the first place. After the coachee has attended the training course though, they should be able to answer that question, and the coach can then go on to ask further questions to help them think about the specific detail that they're going to put in to that meeting structure in order to maximise the chances of success. That's the difference between training and coaching.

Key thought: Coaching, giving feedback and training are different.

Some might argue that 'sales coaching' is all about helping the salesperson to become more effective, so telling, directing, training and giving feedback are all in fact coaching. No they are not. Coaching is coaching and providing feedback is providing feedback. Using all of these different methods of communication can indeed contribute to a constructive and positive conversation focused on developing and growing the salesperson so that they become more effective. This does not though mean that they all become components of coaching.

Giving feedback can most certainly support the ability of the Sales Manager to coach, but it is not coaching. For example, when reviewing a face-to-face meeting, when asked a question about what the customer did when the salesperson began to utilise a piece of visual support, the salesperson may genuinely have no idea at all about what happened. So that's the point in the coaching conversation that feedback can be provided, by the Sales Manager saying: "*OK, well let me help… the customer changed their posture, leant forward, and their arms which previously were folded, unfolded. They also asked three questions about what you were describing…*" That's feedback. It's not coaching. But it does support the coaching process as it allows the Sales Manager to then return to a coaching focused approach and ask: "*So what might that suggest in terms of how the customer was feeling and thinking?*"

So coaching is an activity which aims to provoke the coachee to think, and so to arrive at their own conclusions rather than have the coach (in our context the Sales Manager) do their thinking and their work for them. This isn't to say that the coach doesn't do any thinking or any work – in fact quite the opposite. A skilled coach does an immense amount of thinking - about what the coachee is saying, what questions will best help the process move forward and how to ensure that they remain in the impartial role of coach rather than become a 'teller' of how to do it. And at the same time employing active listening skills, to not only hear everything, but to employ verbal and non-verbal skills to show that everything is being heard (i.e. active listening). Achieving all this requires a lot of concentration and is actually quite hard work. And it is about the coach doing this work for the coachee… but it's not about doing the coachee's work for the coachee!

It is of course a lot easier to simply 'tell' people in the sales team what to do, and can certainly be a lot less time consuming too. This approach though doesn't help people to learn; people learn principally by doing, experiencing, and thinking for themselves. Satellite navigation systems ('sat navs') demonstrate this remarkably well. Use sat nav to travel somewhere, and the chances are that you'll need to use your sat nav next time you go there too. This is because first time around you didn't have to do any thinking, and so you didn't learn about the route for the journey. If the next time you need to travel to this same destination your sat nav for some reason isn't working, you'll have a problem! Without the sat nav there to provide direction, you simply won't know what to do.

If though the first time you travel there you review the alternative routes beforehand with the assistance of a map, work out what the best route is, and then actually navigate during the journey for yourself, the chances of being able to recall how to drive to the location unaided the next time you need to travel to that same destination would increase dramatically - because you've learned by having to think about it rather than been told what to do. You've *reviewed* the map and options, *learned* which route is going to work best, and then *planned* the journey – it's the learning cycle in operation!

And this is why adopting a directing approach is not a good way of developing the abilities of the sales team: you are generating the situation where the team needs you to always be there to tell them what to do.

> **Key thought: 'Telling' might save time now, but in the longer-term it can be actually more time-consuming than if a coaching approach was adopted in the first place.**

All of which should (I hope) begin to question in the minds of those reading this book how much of the time the sales team are 'told' what to do, and how much of the time they are provoked to work it out for themselves. What sort of environment are you creating as a Sales Manager – one where the sales team routinely thinks and so learns, or one where the sales team are routinely 'told'?

Even more importantly, when the sales team are consistently told what to do, they are 'trained' over time that the Sales Manager will do their thinking for them. So when faced with a challenge or problem they will automatically wait to be told what to do rather than work things out for themselves. In other words, this approach develops the environment which encourages sales teams to move to the 'no learn cycle'. This impedes learning, which in turn impedes the ongoing growth of effective selling behaviours (the Inputs), which in turn negatively impacts on sales (the Outputs). At fear of stating the obvious, this does not help the Sales Manager achieve their Job Purpose of *achieving sales through others*.

Clearly, the establishment of a culture which <u>promotes</u> thinking, learning, and the implementation of lessons learned, is a culture which is likely to drive sales success. And as the studies referenced above testify, in the real world coaching does indeed drive higher levels of sales success.

Key thought: What culture are you driving in your sales team? One where the team wait to be told what to do, or one where they are constantly thinking for themselves?

Adopting a coaching based approach provides the Sales Manager with numerous other benefits too. These include...

☺ Because it's the salesperson who plans for future occasions, it is they who own the solution, which makes it more likely that they will want to implement it.

☺ Because it's the salesperson who has reviewed and learned, they understand the logic and reasons to implement the solution – which again means that they are more likely to implement this solution.

☺ When the Sales Manager does nothing other than 'tell', then the sales team's ability will be limited by what the Sales Manager knows and the Sales Manager's ability to review and learn. Coaching unleashes the thinking and learning power of the whole team. This means that the coachee might develop new and more effective ideas and approaches the Sales Manager has never thought of or experienced before.

☺ The relationship between the Sales Manager and the salesperson is enhanced, since this approach helps them to work more as equals; the relationship moves towards one typified by a feeling of synergistic problem solving rather than one of command and control.

☺ When implemented consistently, coaching becomes the thinking style that individuals tend to adopt when the Sales Manager isn't there, and they begin to self-coach. This means that the sales team is perpetually learning and increasing the quality of their Inputs... with of course a consequential positive impact on their Outputs. This last point is of high relevance to field based sales teams, and in particular those based long distances away from the Sales Manager (though just as relevant to internal sales teams too).

Learning how to coach – some key thoughts

A few comments first of all to ensure there are realistic expectations from reading this section:

1) You don't learn how to swim by reading a book; the way to learn how to swim is to actually jump into a swimming pool and to gain a feel for what swimming is all about. The same principle is true of *any* skill, including coaching. It's recommended therefore that Sales Managers wanting to develop coaching skills enlist the help of an appropriately qualified trainer to help, and to learn experientially.

2) When learning how to swim, it's not a good idea to start off by leaping into the deep end of a swimming pool without any buoyancy aids, and then finding out if you can make it to the shallow end without drowning! There is at least a chance of surviving the experience, though if you do survive it won't be without a lot of stress. And you'll probably relive in your mind this unhappy experience every time you return to a swimming pool in the future. So don't try to use newly acquired coaching skills for the first time with the most difficult circumstances, or with the most challenging salesperson in the team. Begin with something very easy, simple and straightforward, where it doesn't matter if it doesn't go quite right, and build up your confidence and skills from there.

It's rather like learning how to juggle... the best way to begin is by throwing just one ball from one hand to the other and back again. This is easy, provides a 'feel' for what juggling is about, and helps to build confidence. It doesn't matter too much if you drop the ball while you're beginning to develop the skill either. It's certainly not recommended that you learn how to juggle by beginning with three fiery torches or three working chain saws!

> **Key thought: You don't learn how to swim by listening to a lecture about it...**

3) Coaching is an enormous subject, indeed so much so that there are formal qualifications available which recognise differing levels of expertise and ability. Allocating just one part of this book to the subject can only provide a 'flavour' of what coaching is all about. It's therefore recommended that Sales Managers read other resources, conduct further research via the Internet, and if they haven't already done so, enlist themselves on a formal training course of a quality appropriate to the professionalism and standards of them and their team.

> **Key thought: The book "Coaching for Performance" by John Whitmore(12) provides a comprehensive introduction to this important skill.**

It's also important to remember that coaching is as much a mind-set as it is a technique. There are times when a lengthy and carefully structured coaching meeting will be appropriate and indeed will be the preferred option of both the coach and coachee – for example, when the salesperson and Sales Manager together invest time to review how well a key account is being managed. Equally, there will be times when the Sales Manager is approached for help, and rather than immediately 'tell' the salesperson what to do will instead adopt a more coaching oriented approach by asking for the salesperson's ideas and then help them to critically evaluate these ideas in order to identify the most appropriate course of action to take. This is a lot shorter than a 'formal' coaching meeting, and may include only some elements of a coaching model. It is none-the-less though a valid approach, and one that continues to promote a coaching and learning culture within the business.

How to coach...

There are a number of coaching models which are suitable and appropriate for use by Sales Managers. A particularly well know model that is explained and described in John Whitmore's book "Coaching for Performance"(12) is GROW, an acronym which stands for **G**oal, **R**eality, **O**ption, and **W**ill. It is a methodology which is structured, yet still provides ample scope for the coach to flex and amend their approach in accordance with the tone and content of the coaching conversation. The four stages of the model are...

Goal
- ✓ The beginning of the session
- ✓ Identifies what the coachee wants to achieve in the long term
- ✓ Identifies what the coachee wants to achieve as a consequence of this coaching conversation
- ✓ Sets short-term goals
- ✓ Sets long-term goals
- ✓ Agrees on what 'success' will look like when it's achieved

Reality
- ✓ Challenges beliefs

✓ Reviews and checks assumptions
✓ Reviews historical situation and background
✓ Identifies what might influence achievement of objectives

Option

✓ Identifies and reviews alternative courses of action
✓ Considers objectively the pros and cons of these alternatives
✓ Considers what might influence success of alternatives
✓ Dispassionately considers the pros and cons of the choices

Will

✓ Agree on actions and time-lines
✓ Agree on follow-up
✓ Identify any support that may be required
✓ Explore benefits of successful implementation
✓ Provide a Vision for success

Whilst GROW might appear to be a 'linear' model, it might be (and more often is) that the coach moves backwards and forwards through the model in response to what transpires during the conversation.

For example, when discussing **Options**, an idea might arise that is so effective that a subsequent check back on reality tells the coachee that the initial **Goal** was not in fact as stretching as it could have been. The requirement therefore could be to return to the 'beginning' of the model and set a more challenging **Goal**.

Equally, it could be that when considering the pros and cons of a potential solution, that a new issue which represents a barrier to success is identified that had not been thought of before, and it's of such significance that it's obvious that the **Goal** that's been set is not realistic. There's an obvious need in these circumstances to return to the 'beginning' of the model again and modify the **Goal** in order to make it realistic.

Or another example might be when exploring what support will best help the coachee to implement the plan of action they've agreed (during the **Will** stage), the coachee suggests engaging the support of a colleague, and when mentioning their name suddenly remembers: "...*I've just remembered, they've actually been on a course about this themselves... maybe they could take time out to provide me some input...*" In which case a return to review this newly thought of course of action as one of the **Options** would be appropriate.

The GROW model can certainly be utilised by Sales Managers to structure coaching conversations during meetings with individual salespeople to review sales plans, consider how to tackle a particular issue in an account, discuss career development, etc.

> **Key thought: The GROW model is a broad structure and not a script; it's the conversation with the coachee which brings this structure to life.**

The model can also be adapted to help the salesperson learn from their everyday experiences. The most obvious context for is when the Sales Manager helps the salesperson review what happened during a customer meeting. In this situation the GROW model might be something like:

GOAL: Agreement on the purpose of the post-customer meeting discussion. This is likely to be about identifying what to do the same / differently on future occasions in order to continually increase the quality of the salesperson's Inputs, and will ideally be focused on one specific facet of selling skills – managing concerns for example.

REALITY: So is the goal realistic? Are the concerns that arose during the customer meeting the 'typical' ones that arise on a day-to-day basis? Is this customer representative of a proportion of customers who are met, or even representative of customers *per se*? Is there sufficient time between now and the next customer meeting to complete the coaching conversation?

OPTION: How was each of the concerns handled? What words were used, and how did the customer respond to what was said in terms of verbal and non-verbal communication? What other facts could have been used to bolster the response? What other proof could have been used to support how the concern was managed? What alternative ways could the concerns have been handled? Why might each of these ideas work better? Or indeed not work better?

WILL: What preparation is required so that the selected way(s) of managing concerns in the future can be implemented effectively? What materials need to be available to support the salesperson's response? What customer responses will demonstrate that the concerns have been managed successfully? How will this support achievement of the meeting's objective(s) and the further development of the relationship with the customer?

In essence then, the GROW model of coaching is helping the salesperson move through the learning cycle, by **reviewing** what happened during the interaction with the customer and how the customer responded, **learning** as a consequence what worked well and what could have been done better and how alternative approaches may have worked more effectively, and then **planning** what to do in the future.

It's important to note that a skilled coach does not slavishly follow a sequence of questions irrespective of what the salesperson has said and how the conversation is progressing; it could be that the conversation moves forward and backwards through the GROW model simply because that is the most effective and conversational way of provoking thought and supporting learning. For example...

Sales Manager: "*OK John, let's review that call to see what we can gain in terms of ideas so that we can ensure the next customer meeting after lunch achieves what you would really like it to.*"

Salesperson: "*Sure!*"

Sales Manager: "*Well, let's start off by considering whether you achieved what you wanted to or not – remind me, what were your objectives for this meeting again?*"

[NB the Sales Manager is already asking questions rather than telling, which would have been an easy thing to do here when firstly reviewing the objectives for the call.]

Salesperson: "*As I explained earlier, the key issue with this particular customer is that he's been disappointed on a couple of occasions with the reliability of our deliveries. So I wanted to reassure him about the new processes we've put in place to better manage them. I also wanted to gain a commitment for ongoing orders on the back of this.*"

Sales Manager: "*And how did you do?*"

Salesperson: "*Well, I thought things went OK. We came away with that order I wanted, and he did seem to be comfortable about what I told him.*"

Sales Manager: "*Yes, that's the way I felt too. So let's see if we can pin down precisely what you did when managing the deliveries issue, because if we can identify why it went so "right" today, you'll have some* *good ideas you can use if a similar situation crops up again in the future. So how did you introduce the subject?"*

[A discussion would ensue here with the Sales Manager asking questions to help the coachee relive the interaction, and to critically evaluate what worked well and what didn't. Even when a meeting has been implemented effectively, it's dangerous to assume that it's not possible to implement a similar meeting *even more* effectively in the future. Hence it would still be important for the Sales Manager to ask questions such as...]

Sales Manager: "...*OK, that did work well for you. Even so, there might be even more effective ways of achieving the same thing; how else could you have handled that?"*

Salesperson: "*How else? That's a tricky one... let me think about this for a moment...*"

[a second alternative is then thought of and described to the manager].

Sales Manager: "*I wonder how well that one would work... what are the reasons that this idea would work, and what do you think are the reasons why it wouldn't?*"

[a discussion then ensues around this idea with the coach (Sales Manager) asking questions to help the coachee critically evaluate the idea and how well it can be applied to similar circumstances in the future.]

Salesperson: "*So, having thought about it I don't think this idea would work as well as what I actually did.*"

Sales Manager: "*OK - it's important though to always make sure there isn't a better way, and I think you've just done a good job of doing this. Are there any circumstances or situations where you think this second idea you've had <u>would</u> work better?*"

Salesperson: "*Actually, I was just beginning to think about maybe using this approach with people who are more analytical than the customer we've just met – they might actually prefer this second approach a little more.*"

Sales Manager: "*What makes you say that?*"

[...and so the Sales Manager again has the opportunity to help the coachee think through how "right" their thoughts are. After due consideration the conversation may continue...]

Salesperson: "*Great! I'm happy with that – I can see how this will help me with the appointments we've got this afternoon.*"

Sales Manager: "*Yes, me too. So let's just summarise: so what exactly are you planning to do, and what's going to prompt you during the discussion with the customer to do these things?*"

[note that it's the coachee who is doing the summing up here – not the coach. That way it's the coachee who has a clear understanding – and more importantly the ownership – of the conclusions that have been reached.]

Sales Manager: "*Fine. We haven't yet though touched on how you used the new brochure that was distributed last week – what are your feelings about that?*"

[i.e. having drawn the discussion about one issue to a conclusion, the Sales Manager is now opening up the coaching conversation again to provoke thought about another key issue...]

Of course, it would have been a lot quicker for the Sales Manager in the above scenario to simply say: "*Good call John – but can I give you a couple of ideas about how you could have done things differently and in particular how to better use the new brochure...*". The focus of Sales Management though should not be to do things quickly – it should be to do things **effectively**, and to effectively *achieve sales through others* as a consequence. For all of the solid theoretical reasons discussed earlier, and because we know it's what the more successful Sales Managers and sales organisations do, the unequivocal recommendation is to implement a coaching style of management whenever possible (which should be for the vast majority of the time).

See Appendix 1. for examples of questions that can be used when implementing the GROW coaching model.

Feedback

Feedback is a means of providing the recipient with objective information about the behaviours they are using and/or the impact these behaviours are having on themselves and/or others. So this is a tool that the Sales Manager can use to 'put in', and is normally used when the other party is lacking this information, and it's the lack of this information that is impeding their ability to improve their Inputs.

A key word in the above description is 'objective', which is a statement of fact, and the opposite of subjective, which is a statement of interpretation and opinion. The examples of subjective and objective statements in Table 2. Illustrate this example well...

Subjective feedback can be problematical for a number of reasons. The first of these is that because it is opinion it can be disagreed and argued with. So if a salesperson is told by their manager that they are

Subjective	Objective
"The customer didn't like you."	"During the meeting the customer's posture changed. They sat back in their chair, folded their arms, and at the end of the meeting stated that they would meet with another representative from our company, but did not want to meet again with you."
"Your closing skills are poor."	"For every ten face-to-face meetings you conduct, you are gaining on average 1 commitment, compared to the average for the team of 3.5 for each 10 face-to-face meetings conducted."
"You're not punctual."	"Our office hours begin at 9.00am, and on the last 10 working days the earliest you've arrived at your desk is 9.23am."
"The report you submitted was great!"	"The report you submitted answered all the questions, utilised bullet points and summaries as appropriate, and included a summary of the key messages you wanted to communicate at the end of each section."
"You did a great job of that meeting…"	"The meeting structure was aligned perfectly to the structure we provide on our internal sales training programme. The questions you asked resulted in the customer listing their key needs, and you presented relevant features and the associated benefits so that the customer understood how the product addressed their needs. And on conclusion of the meeting the customer placed the order."

Table 2. Some examples of subjective and objective feedback

not punctual, the likelihood is that the response will be: "*Yes I am!*". And this sort of situation can quickly deteriorate into a 'my opinion is, versus your opinion is', situation.

Moreover, if the subjective feedback is about the person, such as "*Your closing skills are poor*", then this is likely to be perceived as (at best) critical. In fact, so much so that it will feel like an 'attack', and the normal reaction to an attack is to either attack back or to retreat and withdraw. So the response to what may well be perceived to be an attack on an individual's closing skills might be "*My closing skills are poor?! How would you know – you don't even sell! And right now I'm the only person in the team who's on target – what about everyone else?!*" At fear of stating the obvious, this is not conducive to a constructive Sales Manager – salesperson relationship! And if the salesperson goes quiet, withdraws, and simply ignores what's been said then that's not good news either.

> **Key thought: Subjective feedback is opinion. Objective feedback is based on facts.**

Because subjective feedback is opinion (and so not about behaviours), it also provides no guidance regarding what behaviours should be used in the future. So telling someone that "your closing skills are poor" provides no indication of what needs to be done differently in order to become more effective; it's only providing the opinion that skill levels are not what they should be. This is true of positive subjective feedback too. Telling a salesperson that the report they submitted was "…great", or that they did a "great job of the meeting" provides no indication about why the report was great, or what they did during the meeting to make it great. So whilst positive subjective feedback might provide a salesperson with a bit of warm glow inside, it provides no guidance regarding what they need to do in the future to achieve a similar positive result.

Objective feedback is based on facts. For a Sales Manager focused on developing the skills of the sales team, this means that feedback is normally based on behaviours... what the salesperson said or did, and/or what the customer said or did. Objective feedback can't be argued with; it's difficult to argue with a manager who states a fact such as "*Our office hours begin at 9.00am, and on the last 10 working days the earliest you've arrived at your desk is 9.23am*".

Objective feedback is not about the person, it's about behaviours, and so when focused on the salesperson's behaviours is less likely to be perceived as a personal attack. And it prevents the situation where the Sales Manager might make an incorrect interpretation. For example, it might well be true that "*...for every ten face-to-face meetings you conduct, you are gaining on average 1 commitment. The average for the team as a whole is 3.5 commitments for each 10 face-to-face meetings conducted*". But this does not automatically mean that the individual concerned has poor closing skills. It might. Or it might mean that they need to better qualify opportunities, as too many low chance opportunities are being pursued right now.

So the message is a simple one: **When providing feedback, avoid subjectivity.**

Having said that, if the *only* language that's used is objective, then the conversation will become cold, overly-structured and robotic. So including within the conversation subjective feedback is OK, just as long as that subjectivity is further qualified by objective facts. There's absolutely nothing wrong in saying during a conversation which is reviewing a meeting with a customer: "*Well the customer seemed to be really comfortable about your suggestion there...* (subjective) *...to have immediately phoned the operations director to gain agreement to move forward and then finance to provide you with a purchase order number...* (objective) *...is probably about as positive a result as you could achieve!*"

Objective feedback can also be about the impact on others, and is appropriate to provide when an individual does not have this information. For example:
"*...an order this late means that production can't add it into this week's schedule.*"
"*...an order this late means that the rescheduling puts an extra £200 cost on delivery which impacts on the profitability we achieve with this key account.*"
"*...that lack of information means that the underwriters cannot satisfy company policy without asking you for clarification, which impacts on how quickly the deal can be done.*"

> **Key thought: Coaching is about enjoying a constructive conversation; avoid sounding like a robot!**

Feedback – when to provide it

One of the main times to provide feedback is when addressing unacceptable behaviours within the business, and this is discussed in some depth in Book 6. of this series: "Sales Management: Leading the sales team". Here, we will focus on the subject of this book… *developing the skills of the sales team*.

We have already discussed how coaching is a tool that can be used to help the coachee review an experience they've already had, or indeed an experience they are going to have – and so to help them plan what to do in order to achieve success. Sometimes though, the coachee lacks the information required in order to be able to review. This is the point where providing the relevant information objectively, and so providing feedback is constructive.

For example, when reviewing what happened during a face-to-face sales discussion, the Sales Manager might ask: "*So what did the customer do when you brought out the brochure and provided them with that information?*" the salesperson might answer "…*I'm sorry, I really didn't notice*" – which means that they don't have the information required in order to assess whether what they did was appropriate or not. This is when feedback can help. So the Sales Manager might say: "*Well, she unfolded her arms, then sat forward, engaged you in eye contact, and asked if she could take the brochure from you to read more about the Case Study in the brochure you highlighted*". That's feedback. And from there it's easy to return to a more coaching style of conversation and ask: "…*so how would you interpret that?*"

Another example would be when pre-coaching to help a salesperson prepare for a meeting with a customer, when the Sales Manager could ask: "*So what paperwork do you need to have with you so that the order can be dispatched asap?*" and the salesperson responds: "*I don't know!*" In which case the Sales Manager might say: "*With the increased sensitivities around audit, the orders you've submitted over the last 3 weeks that have not included pro-forma PF135 completed and signed by the customer have been delayed by up to a week*". That's feedback. And from there it's easy to return to a more coaching style of conversation and ask: "*...so how can you introduce this requirement into the conversation with this customer?*"

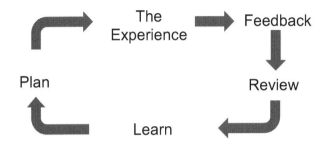

figure 10. How feedback can support The Learning Cycle

Coaching inexperienced salespeople

Whilst the principles of coaching can be applied similarly to salespeople no matter what their levels of experience, there are some particularly important points and principles that are important to the coaching of those who are less experienced.

The first of these relates to confidence – an important part of the 'Attitude' leg of the Knowledge-Skills-Attitude stool described earlier. By definition, the levels of skills and knowledge in an inexperienced salesperson will be relatively low – this is why it's important for the sales manager to help them maintain confidence levels – it's the leg of the three-legged stool which will help them rise to the challenges they face as they develop skills and know-how via experience.

So whilst it's always important to focus on positive behaviours and the positive consequences these behaviours have achieved as well as helping the salesperson to correct less positive things with *all* salespeople, it is particularly important to do this when coaching the less experienced. When I first moved into a training role my new manager, someone with immense experience in the world of training & development, summed it up beautifully: "*Catch them doing it right – Praise Pays!*".

Key thought: Coaching effectively can help to build the intangible but critical issue of confidence.

This does not mean of course *only* praising and so potentially developing a false and unrealistic sense of security and success. It does mean though ensuring that there is a good and positive balance between consideration of what went well, and what could have gone better. The corollary of this is to only find things that the salesperson is doing wrong in order to 'develop' them – which is what's referred to as 'find a fault management'. The consequence of this approach will be that the sales team learn very quickly to avoid coaching and so to avoid contact with the Sales Manager (and quite reasonably too!).

Inexperienced salespeople by definition have less experiences to draw on, and so are less likely to be able to consider other alternative ways of managing situations when asked questions such as "*...OK, so how else could you have managed that situation?*". Indeed, sometimes they may not be able to think of any alternative ways at all. In such situations the coach might be tempted to tell them the 'right' answer – but doing this is not coaching. A better way is to provide input by giving the salesperson a number of alternative solutions, and then once again move back into a coaching style by asking the salesperson to now critically evaluate these alternatives, and so come to a conclusion independently about which might work best for them. For example...

Sales manager: "...*OK, so how else could you have handled that?*"

[pause]

Salesperson: "*you know, I really don't know. I've never come across this situation before and I'm struggling to think what else I could possibly do...*"

Sales manager: "*Well, there are a number of different ideas I've seen people use over the years. I can tell you what these are, and then I think we should think through together how well each of them might suit you and this sort of situation.*"

[the manager then outlines a number of alternatives – not why they are and are not appropriate, but simply describes the alternatives themselves.]

Sales manager: "*So that's what I've seen... let's have a think about these and, as I say, in particular how they might suit you and this sort of situation. Let's take the first one – what do you like about that, why might that one work for you...*"

[the sales manager, having given the options, now let's the coachee take ownership of their critical evaluation.]

Following this strategy, what quite often happens is that the salesperson either begins to modify these ideas, or is even prompted to think up an entirely new option over and above those the Sales Manager has inputted to the conversation. And of course either of these outcomes is good news!

When adopting this approach of providing alternatives for the salesperson to critically evaluate, it's important to ensure that the manager doesn't give away which of the alternatives they prefer. So aim to use about the same amount of words to describe each, use about the same voice tone when describing each of them, and also reinforce what's been said with the same level of expressive body language.

The other way of managing the situation where the salesperson isn't able to think of any alternative options is to ask what might initially seem to be quite a bizarre question… but is one that does actually work quite well: "*OK, but imagine for a moment you <u>did</u> know what the answer is – what would it be*?". Try it – you'll be amazed at the number of times the salesperson all of a sudden knows what 'the answer' is!

When not to coach

There are specific times and circumstances when a more directive and telling style is more appropriate than a coaching style. These include:

- To comply with legislation. In financial services for example, there are specific tasks which need to be completed during the sales process to ensure that the selling organisation has complied with local legislative requirements. These are not open to discussion – so clear direction from the Sales Manager regarding what must and must not be done is important.

- When initially providing training. Here the requirement is to 'put in', particularly when passing on what we refer to as 'best practice'. Hence the 'pulling out' style of coaching is inappropriate – you can't 'pull out' unless something has been 'put in' to begin with. Coaching becomes appropriate *after* training to help the individual think about how they are implementing and applying what they have learned.

- When addressing issues and/or behaviours that are unacceptable in the workplace and need to be changed. This is another area which is not open to discussion.

- When the consequences of the task being completed incorrectly are unacceptable. Though having said that, a lot of these occasions will either require training (Input), or require the Sales Manager to coach in advance of the event – so the coachee has thought through everything they need to and are fully prepared to complete the task effectively.

How does the Sales Manager know what to coach?

Although this is only one question, the best way to answer it is to break this down into three different questions as follows...

1) **How does the sales manager know what the salesperson has done 'right' during an observed sales discussion and what could have been done better?**

The answer to this question can be explained by the very simple diagram in figure 11.

Behaviour → Consequences

figure 11. The simple equation that drives the coaching conversation

Remember that coaching is not about the manager expressing their opinion, or telling the salesperson what to do. It is about helping the salesperson *review* what they have done, as a consequence to *learn*, and so be able to *plan* how to improve the quality of their Inputs (coaching can be used in more scenarios than this, but we will concentrate here on the role of the Sales Manager as a sales coach). The best way to help the salesperson critically evaluate their effectiveness is to not only ask them about what they have done, but to also ask them about what happened *because* of what they did; or to use the more precise language in figure 11., to focus on the *consequences* of their behaviour rather than the behaviour itself.

> **Key thought: a behaviour is what someone says and/or does; asking an open question, sitting back in a chair, and the tilting of a head to one side are all examples of 'behaviours'.**

For example, the Sales Manager might have noted that the salesperson isn't sending an e-mail in advance of meetings to outline the meeting's purpose, propose an agenda, and to provide information that would be helpful for the customer to have in advance.

94

If the Sales Manager focuses on the salesperson's behaviours and expresses an opinion regarding how 'right' or 'wrong' this approach is, this will have a relatively small amount of influence on the salesperson's behaviours in the future. Simply providing opinion is a relatively weak influencing strategy. Focusing the salesperson instead on the *consequences* of what they are doing (or in this case *not* doing) will help to provoke the coachee to think and evaluate for themselves whether what they are doing is achieving the desired outcome or not. The consequences of failing to make contact in advance of meetings may well be things like the...

*   ...customer needing to leave the meeting to acquire information that's required to support the discussion – which is a waste of time from the salesperson's point of view and reduces the amount of face-to-face time they have with the customer when on their premises.

*   ...conversation needing to be postponed altogether pending the customer acquiring the information.

*   ...customer not understanding fully the purpose of the meeting and so not setting aside sufficient time for the meeting's objectives to be achieved.

*   ...customer failing to invite relevant stakeholders to the meeting as they didn't understand the relevance of the meeting to them – which slows down the decision making process.

...and it is these consequences that the manager needs to focus the thoughts of the salesperson on during the coaching conversation. This could be done by asking questions such as:

"What happened when you asked the customer for the information you needed? How long were we left waiting? How did this impact on the meeting? What would you have preferred to have happened? What else could you have done to achieve this more desired result?"

"What impact will the postponement have on your sales pipeline? How important was it for the sale to have been concluded today? Why didn't this happen? What else could you have done to prevent this delay?"

"How did the customer not understanding the purpose of the meeting affect the outcome? What impact will this have on your sales pipeline? How important was it for the sale to have been concluded today? Why didn't this happen? Why didn't the customer understand the purpose of the meeting? What else could you have done to prevent this delay?"

Key thought: The opinion of the coach is irrelevant. It's the coach's duty to help the coachee work out <u>for themselves</u> what's good and not so good by helping them to think through the *consequences* of behaviours.

When employed as a full time field-based coach in the early part of my career (as part of the training team), I remember distinctly one of the first field-based coaching days I conducted with a representative responsible for a geographical area over the East side of England. During one of the customer meetings I joined her for, I felt distinctly uncomfortable because of what she was doing... the words she was using, and the style she was adopting was by no means the same as the words and style I would have employed in the same situation. This meeting was to be an important learning experience for me though, because what I also noted was the reaction of the customer – both verbally and body language wise. It was all very positive. The key learning point for me was: just because someone does 'it' a different way to me, doesn't necessarily mean that they are doing 'it' wrong. It means they are doing 'it' differently. We all have different personalities and styles, and what suits one person doesn't necessarily suit another. What *is* important though is that it suits the customer, and the best way of understanding how well 'it' is suiting the customer is by observing how the customer reacts... i.e. the consequences of the salesperson's behaviours.

2) **How does the sales manager know what behaviours the salesperson *should* be using, i.e. which ones *are known* to be high quality Inputs, and so are most likely to lead to the achievement of the desired Outputs?**

This second question overlaps with the first, since the wrong answer would most definitely be "*the right way is the way I used to do it when I was a salesperson!*".

It does make sense though to ensure that all in the sales team are armed with an understanding of the behaviours that we know tend to work – the ones that produce the desired response from the customer and so do produce the Outcomes required. A clear description of what these Inputs are, are what's referred to as **sales standards**.

Sales standards provide a template for success. They should not though be a straight jacket that prevents the salesperson from being able to express their personality, and so bring the meeting or telephone conversation with a customer to life. They should all the same though provide a clear framework within which the salesperson operates. For example, the sending of an e-mail on all appropriate occasions to outline the purpose of the meeting, propose an agenda for the discussion, and to confirm the timing in advance of the meeting, is a clear standard. It doesn't say what words are going to be used, or what style the communication is going to adopt – which means that the salesperson has not been forced into a proverbial straight jacket. It does though make it clear what 'good practice' is, and so what the expectations of the Sales Manager are.

When someone new joins the sales team, it's important that they are provided an understanding of the sales standards the organisation has, and clarity regarding the Sales Manager's expectations regarding how these standards are going to be adopted. This can be achieved via initial sales training (for a total newcomer to sales), induction training, and via one-to-one meetings with the Sales Manager. Put very simply, this is a description of 'the way we do things around here'. And these are the things that are 'done around here' because it's known that when they are done, the desired results tend to happen.

This might sound very simple and very logical... which it is. But this does provoke three very important questions: 1) does your organisation know what sales standards drive success? 2) does the sales team know and understand what these are? and finally 3) assuming a positive answer to the second question, are they doing these things routinely? The only way that question 3) can be answered is by observing first-hand what the sales team is really doing in the real world. For internal sales teams this means listening to 'live' calls or reviewing recorded calls with the salesperson, and for field based Sales Managers it means conducting field based coaching.

For those reading this book who work in organisations that do not yet have a recognised set of sales standards and see the potential benefits of them, the good news is that there is an easy way of gaining access to a set of generic sales standards, and at no cost. In 2001 the UK government formed a body called the Marketing and Sales Standards Setting Body – the MSSSB. This body was given the remit of developing 'National Occupational Standards' for the sales and marketing professions of the UK – in very simple terms, a description of what we know successful sales and marketing professionals do – the Inputs that drive success. The work on these was completed in 2006 and can be downloaded at no charge from www.cfa.uk.com/standards/marketing-and-sales.html (correct at time of going to press).

figure 12. The UK National Occupational Standards in Sales – in CD format

The National Occupational Standards in Sales (NOS) cover all professional selling roles, including telesales, field based sales, Sales Manager, key account manager, and global account manager. The NOS can be used to inform job descriptions, help with TNAs, and indeed support any task which requires an understanding of what the sales team (including the Sales Manager) needs to do to create success. Indeed, the UK NOS have proved sufficiently useful for some organisations to now be using these as the basis of their sales standards for all their sales teams globally.

Key thought: The National Occupational Standards in Sales are a clear description of the Inputs required to make sales success happen.

With no apologies for again emphasising the importance of understanding what Inputs are required, take a look at the statements in Tables 3. and 4. Depending on whether you manage an internal or field based sales team, how well does your team measure up against these? If you have any less than 10 x YES's, then this means that the team has a degree of uncertainty about the Inputs required for success – the opposite of role clarity, which we know relates to higher levels of sales success. This is not conducive to the Sales Manager achieving their Job Purpose of *achieving sales through others...*

3) **Which salesperson behaviours should be addressed during the coaching conversation?**

(...this question applies to face-to-face meetings, telephone based conversations, presentations – all types of customer interactions.)

Coaching is about helping the salesperson to learn, which logically means that the coaching conversation after the customer interaction should include

Each person in the sales team can describe...	
...how to structure the appointment winning telephone call.	YES / NO
...how to structure a face-to-face meeting with a prospect / customer.	YES / NO
...the key elements that should be included at the beginning of the meeting to capture interest and focus attention.	YES / NO
...the key elements that should be employed when drawing the meeting to a close and gaining a commitment.	YES / NO
...the structure to follow when managing customer concerns so that not only is the relevant information provided, but the emotion behind the concern is managed too.	YES / NO
...the guidelines that govern effective use of Visual Support.	YES / NO
...what non-verbal communication (body language) used by the customer needs to be observed in order to assess their level of interest in the sales presentation.	YES / NO
...how to qualify opportunities in order that time is invested in the most effective way possible.	YES / NO
...the key rules and guidelines that govern the writing of effective proposals (the key do's and don'ts).	YES / NO

Table 3. Some of the key Inputs for field based sales professionals

Each person in the sales team can describe...	
...how to structure the opening to an outbound sales call.	YES / NO
...the key elements that should be included in the critical first few seconds of the conversation to capture interest and win the right to continue the call.	YES / NO
...how to qualify the call to ensure that the person being spoken with has either the power to make the purchasing decision or influence it.	YES / NO
...the key elements that should be employed when drawing the conversation to a close and gaining a commitment.	YES / NO
...the structure to follow when managing customer concerns so that not only is the relevant information provided, but the emotion behind the concern is managed too.	YES / NO
...how to utilise voice to communicate both confidence and conviction.	YES / NO
...how to qualify opportunities in order that time is invested in the most effective way possible.	YES / NO
...the key rules and guidelines that govern the writing of effective proposals (the key do's and don'ts).	YES / NO

Table 4. Some of the key Inputs for internal sales professionals

consideration of which parts of the meeting went well *as well as* which parts could potentially have been conducted better. So a possible answer to this question could be: "*all of them*".

"*All of them*" is most definitely the wrong answer though. This would require an enormous amount of time and would require discussion on so many issues that the salesperson's thinking on any one issue would have only limited time and so lack depth. The number of issues discussed would probably result in both confusion and a lack of clarity regarding what they actually should do more of / less of / differently to achieve a more desirable result. And the salesperson would probably feel pretty bored and disenchanted with a conversation as laborious as this too. Logically therefore the sales coach needs to be *selective* about the issues that are discussed.

The ideal is for the focus of the coaching conversation to have been agreed before the interaction rather than thought about afterwards. This fits well the philosophy behind the GROW model, as the salesperson can be asked in advance of the interaction to think about the specific area(s) of their skill set they want to develop, and so ask the observing coach to concentrate in particular on these behaviours and the consequences of these behaviours. This means that the post customer interaction coaching conversation can begin by the coach asking questions such as: "*So remind me, what exactly is it that our conversation needs to focus on...*" and so refocus on the Goal of the coaching conversation. This approach is also beneficial for the observing sales coach, as they can concentrate on observing the parts of the meeting that are relevant to the skill area the salesperson has asked them to focus on in particular. Remembering every nuance of verbal and non-verbal communication, by both the salesperson and the customer, so that the interaction can be reviewed afterwards, is far from easy (understatement!) A lot easier is to focus principally on just the most important parts of the meeting.

> **Key thought: Focus coaching on priority issues. Don't address everything in one go!**

It's likely though that the Sales Manager will identify other skill areas or issues that could be improved over and above those they've been asked to focus on. If one or more of these are impacting significantly on the salesperson's success, then clearly the coach has a responsibility to draw these in the conversation by including observations of what the customer did or did not do which were less than desirable (the undesirable consequences which signal that the selling behaviours utilised weren't as 'right' as they could have been). Once the salesperson has been provoked to think about these customer behaviours, it would be strange if they *didn't* want to explore why they happened.

It's also worth emphasising again here that coaching is most definitely not just about provoking the coachee to think about what they can do differently; it's just as important to provoke thought about what's already going well – so when the desired result is being achieved, what the behaviours are that the salesperson is utilising in order to achieve this positive result. Positive reinforcement of positive behaviours can help the salesperson to understand what to do more of, more consciously, more often. It's also a great way for the Sales Manager to recognise what the salesperson is already doing well and to help the salesperson feel valued. This will impact positively on motivation, and also help to position in the salesperson's mind that Sales Manager coaching is a positive thing, rather than it being perceived to be about the Sales Manager adopting a 'find a fault management' approach.

As I commented in the section which discussed 360 degree feedback: in my experience, it's ironically the most experienced and successful who are the most self-critical, and who quite often are not totally aware of just how high the quality of Inputs they are employing actually is. Observing them first-hand is both a great opportunity to recognise, and for the Sales Manager to acquire great ideas to pass on to the rest of the team!

Who in the team should the Sales Manager coach?

To answer this question, it's useful to consider the world of sport...

It tends to be the most successful sportspeople who employ the services of a coach – not because they are poor performers, but because once having got to the top, it's very difficult to stay there. They are more than aware that their competition will be working hard to catch up with them, and any slippage in standards, or unwitting introduction of a bad habit can mean that this is what happens. There's a lot of parallels here to the world of sales…

Formula 1 racing teams invest significant amounts of time observing video recordings of practice & qualifying laps, and indeed of actual races in order to identify where every one hundredth of a second can be taken off a lap time by an improvement of the Inputs – what the driver actually does. When competing at this very high level, even the smallest increase in efficiency can mean the difference between a podium place and losing. There are parallels with the world of sales here too.

So the answer to the question of who in the team the sales manager should coach is actually a simple one: everybody, including the high performers. From a business focussed, logical, and pragmatic perspective, improving the performance of a high performer by a very small percentage can sometimes increase their Outputs more than improving the performance of a low performer by a large percentage. Indeed, beware investing an inordinate amount of time in low performers – this is not the best way of achieving the maximum returns from time and effort invested.

Even very well-known players right at the top of their sport work hard to maintain their skills...

"You must respect people and work hard to be in shape. And I used to train very hard. When the other players went to the beach after training, I was there, kicking the ball" (Pele)

"David Beckham is Britain's finest striker of a football not because of a God-given talent but because he practices with a relentless application that the vast majority of less gifted players wouldn't contemplate" (Sir Alex Ferguson commenting on the training ethic of David Beckham)

Adapting coaching style

There are times when adapting coaching style to specific circumstances is entirely appropriate. This subject moves us into the realms of some quite advanced coaching techniques, so the aim of this brief section is to simply highlight what some of these are, so that those who are interested in this greater depth of information can subsequently seek further resources and support...

Different personalities... The most obvious requirement to adapt coaching style is when respecting different personality types. There's a very old saying: "Do unto others as you would have done to yourself", or in more modern language, treat others in the same way as you'd like to be treated yourself. Now as an ethical mind-set about having consideration for others, this is fine. But in terms of communicating with others, it most certainly is not; what suits one personality type does not necessarily suit another. When it comes to communication, the saying should be: "Do unto others as they would like it done to them"!

So when coaching a more reflective personality type who feels comfortable analysing a situation, then there is a need to adapt coaching style accordingly. Asking questions in a way which fails to allow them to think and consider options and alternatives to the extent that they would like is likely to result in the coachee feeling uncomfortable, and at an extreme, even wanting to withdraw from the coaching conversation. The opposite would be true of a high energy, action oriented individual; drawing out the conversation in a way which to them might feel unnecessarily long and detailed could well have the same result.

Having described a couple of obvious scenarios, it will have become apparent that this is no more though than we expect of a professional salesperson: an ability to adapt to the emotional needs of the customer. So if it's OK for us to expect this level of professionalism to be demonstrated by the sales team, then surely it must be OK for the sales team to expect this level of professionalism to be demonstrated by the Sales Manager also...

Having said that, there is also a danger for any and every personality type, that our typical traits become so dominant that they begin to become a little out of control without us realising it. And then, rather than being our inherent strengths, they become *overdone strengths*, and what are often referred to as 'weaknesses'. It's rather like when you listen to music; when the volume is at an 'easy to listen to' level, then we do indeed hear music. Crank up the volume way too high though, and it becomes a bit of a noise! So moving back to the two examples above... a reflective analytical style can become so analytical that they move into analysis paralysis! And a high energy individual who enjoys moving forward quickly can begin to take a 'ready, fire, aim' approach! And both of these situations can impact negatively on a coaching conversation, the former potentially wanting to explore more options to a greater depth than is required and as a consequence not coming to any firm conclusion, and the latter wanting to move ahead having thought of just one alternative way forward, and not having thought through fully the pros and cons of even that one, let alone one or two others.

So whilst it's true that the sales coach has a responsibility to respect and flex to the personality of the coachee, it's also true to say that they have a responsibility to help the coachee retain a control of their personal traits in order to achieve the desired outcome.

Key thought: The Strength Deployment Inventory® (SDI®) is a powerful tool which provides an understanding of emotional drivers, personal strengths and the potential for overdone strengths to impact negatively on performance. For more details see www.personalstrengthspublishing.co.uk

Different cultures... Different cultures of the world have different sets of 'norms' when it comes to communication, and certainly a very different set of attitudes and values. In the APAC Region, societies are more hierarchical than those in EMEA, and the issue of 'face' has a much stronger impact too. It's also accepted in this Region that the best way to learn is to copy those who are already highly successful... those who are recognised as 'masters'. So the attitude of the sales team towards the Sales Manager and to coaching can be very different. The preferred way forward is often to receive advice from the 'master' who is perceived to be higher in the societal hierarchy – so be told what to do – the very opposite of coaching. So structuring of the meeting, the way the conversation is managed, and the wording and subtlety of questions needs to be sensitive to this situation.

This is just one example of how culture can influence coaching style, but of course there are many others. In Europe there are cultural differences even between different countries, with some nationalities enjoying a more structured approach to thinking than others.

Although having said all this, as was stated in chapter 1. as part of the discussion related to how different generations prefer to learn, there are as many differences between individual people within any group as there are between groups. So a blanket statement related to the culture of a given geographical area of the world isn't necessarily true to the same degree with every professional salesperson in that part of the world. It is reasonable though to say that there is a need to be alert to *potential* cultural differences and the way that these differences might impact on coaching style.

Some coaching applications…

Before the event – a lot of the examples provided so far have focused on helping the salesperson to think through what happened during a meeting or telephone conversation with the customer, so they can identify what's gone well and what could have gone better by thinking through the behaviours they employed, and in particular the consequences of these behaviours. In other words, the examples have focused on the salesperson having an **experience**, subsequently **reviewing** that experience, **learning** by considering alternative approaches that could have been adopted, and as a consequence **planning** what to do next time around. Exactly this approach though can be adopted when helping the salesperson *prepare* for experiences.

So following the GROW structure again, the Sales Manager might ask *in advance* of a meeting with a customer:

GOAL: "*So remind me, what exactly do you want to achieve from this meeting? How are the meeting objectives aligned to your business plan? What is your 'fall back' position? What do you want my observations to focus on in particular? What is it going to be most constructive for us to concentrate on during our review afterwards?"*

REALITY: *"Does the person we're meeting have the power to make this decision today? Who else needs to be involved in their decision making process? What is this organisation's normal speed when it comes to making a purchase of this stature? How much does the skill area you want me to focus on impact on your ability to achieve?"*

OPTION: *"What questions are you going to ask to check that the needs you've identified previously are still relevant and of a high priority? How are you planning to describe the product/service in terms of what's relevant to the specific job role this person has? Who else might be at the meeting and what might their needs & requirements be? What internal barriers to implementation is this person likely to need to manage – and what can we do proactively to help them? What other materials do you think it might be useful to have as a contingency?"*

WILL: *"So summarise for me the game-plan you have in mind now... What can I do to support your preparations? When do you need to notify Production about this likely order? How comfortable are you that everything has been thought through to the degree it needs to be thought through?"*

Do note that these questions are just examples, and in the real world the questions that are asked during a coaching conversation about planning and preparation for a customer interaction are going to be far more specific to the situation than this. These examples are purely meant to illustrate how well the GROW model can be applied into this kind of situation... the one where the coach is helping the coachee think through the experience and how best to manage it *in advance* of it happening.

111

> **Key thought: Coaching is not only about reviewing events after they've happened; it's also an approach that can be used to help salespeople think through how they are going to manage events *before* they've happened.**

By consistently coaching before customer interactions, the Sales Manager is also reinforcing their expectations regarding what standard practice should be (I guess we've all come across the 6 x P's.. **P**rior **P**reparation **P**revents **P**retty **P**oor **P**resentation!). Moreover, the more the Sales Manager does this routinely when working with their team, the more that everyone in the sales team will develop the habit of doing this routinely when the Sales Manager is not there too. And isn't that good news?!

When the customer interaction has been successful, this also means that the post-interaction coaching conversation is likely to be biased towards identifying the selling behaviours that have been successful by reviewing their positive consequences – very much a case of 'catching them doing it right'. So the pre-interaction coaching has helped the salesperson increase the quality of their Inputs, which will have enhanced their ability to achieve, and the post-interaction coaching will be reinforcing what a great job they did of implementing the ideas they developed for themselves as part of their professional preparation. Surely this is the best way to encourage the sales team to prepare fully and professionally rather than just directing them to do it?

Coaching 'at distance' - Field based Sales Managers can't be with each of their team every day. Sales Managers with an international remit certainly can't. Indeed, some International Sales Managers may even have the challenge of managing their sales team 'virtualy' 100% of the time. This does not mean though that it's not possible to adopt a coaching approach to managing them.

The unequivocal recommendation is to ensure that whenever possible, the team are spoken with via a visual connection rather than just over the telephone. Easy to use tools such as Webex will facilitate this, though if something as sophisticated as this is not available, simple and free to use tools like Skype or Apple's FaceTime work just as well. Seeing each other's facial gestures will enhance communication, and make the conversation a lot more personable. The opportunity to engage in eye contact certainly makes a difference. There's also the added bonus from the Sales Manager's perspective that this will prevent the salesperson trying to multi-task and do other jobs at the same time, which they could be tempted to do if they were engaged in a normal telephone call! Though there again, if the salesperson does not perceive the coaching conversation to be of high value, and doesn't want to concentrate on it 100%, perhaps it's the Sales Manager who needs to do a better job of selling its benefits.

When coaching 'at distance', exactly the same principles apply as have already been discussed. It's just that this is a conversation between two people who are at different geographical locations rather than in the same place. This physical distance apart though should not impact on the effort and professionalism that the coach puts into ensuring the meeting of minds is structured, impactful, and of high value to the salesperson (and will therefore be of high value to the Sales Manager also).

This was illustrated well by a client of mine a while ago. This business owner described to me how he'd employed two field based salespeople from a competitor organisation. They were both young and 'hungry', and as well as wanting to achieve high results wanted to develop themselves personally. One of the key reasons they left their previous organisation was a lack of contact with their line manager. The feedback he'd received from them a short time into their new jobs was that they were a lot happier, and in particular were very happy about the higher levels of contact they were having.

Interestingly, the dissatisfaction they voiced about levels of contact in their previous roles wasn't so much about the quantity of contact, but more about the quality of contact - their line manager spoke to them almost daily, but it was very much a case of the manager speaking *to* them rather than engaging in a conversation *with* them. What the manager was interested to ask about during the calls he made was sales results and activity plans, so very much a case of checking up with a focus on the agenda of the manager. The new Sales Manager who they'd moved to actually spoke with them *less* frequently than their previous manager, but the focus of the conversation was very different. Their new manager was interested to discuss with them any challenges they had, and to help them to problem solve in advance of meetings with customers. Of course, like any Sales Manager, their new manager was interested to learn about sales figures, but was also constantly engaged in conversations about how they'd achieved their successes. The telephone calls were of longer duration too.

It's interesting that the perception of these two sales professionals was that their previous line manager didn't communicate with them, when in fact his calls were more frequent than those of the new Sales Manager who they were enjoying working for a lot more. This is a graphic example of a critical point:

Making a telephone call does not automatically mean reaching out and communicating with the team. Adopting a salesperson focused, coaching style approach makes a difference!

Making sure conversations 'at distance' are of high quality is also important for two other reasons...

Firstly, working 'at distance' away from the rest of the team can be a lonely job. It's known that having a sense of belonging to a team impacts positively on motivation(13), so it makes good sense for the Sales Manager to invest time to ensure that those who are isolated geographically do not feel isolated from the rest of the team emotionally, and do not feel distant to the company as a whole (this is true for all personality styles, including those who prefer to think and work self-dependently).

Secondly, sales professionals responsible for account management, key account management, and managing the ongoing relationship with customers, vendor partners, wholesalers, and other external organisations, are likely to be natural team-players, and blessed with the attributes that enable them to work as a close team with these customers, partners, and intermediaries. And there-in can lie the problem. Sometimes these abilities and strengths become a little out of control, and that can lead to them feeling more a part of the external team they are responsible for managing, than it does to their own company. And that's dangerous, as it can lead to the salesperson being more sensitive to the needs of others than they are to the requirements of their role and the business. In short, they 'go native'. This can lead to erosion of margin and even Win-Lose negotiations in favour of the other party. Regular quality contact with the Sales Manager can help to prevent this from happening.

Account reviews, Quarterly business reviews, etc.
– Ideal scenarios for a coaching approach. It's all too easy during reviews when the situation is successful to say "*well done*" and "*great job*" without exploring all the reasons <u>why</u> the salesperson has done a great job and done well. Helping the salesperson to highlight these Inputs in their mind will help ensure they do more of the same in the future, and recognise the professional effort they're putting into the job. As well as being a means of recognition, this bolsters both confidence and motivation.

In keeping with the ethos of coaching, it's also worthwhile though considering other options and alternatives. It just might be that the salesperson can think of ways of doing things *even more* effectively. And if they do, they will certainly thank you for that! As a Sales Manager you've added significant value, and of course if the salesperson is achieving more, then so are you...

Career Planning – There's more discussion on this subject in chapter 8. Suffice to say here that this is most definitely a coaching situation. There is also likely to be significant amounts of input from the Sales Manager during these discussions in the form of advising, mentoring, providing information the salesperson wasn't previously aware of, etc. The Sales Manager is likely to have experienced a lot more than the salesperson they are engaging with, so will be aware of a lot more of the opportunities for career development and how to develop the skills and know-how to achieve the desired career development. They're also likely to have observed how large numbers of other salespeople have developed their careers. The old adage 'you don't know what you don't know' is certainly true – which is why the Sales Manager will need to flex during these meetings between the 'drawing out' approach of coaching, and the 'putting in' of information from their own knowledge and experience.

Team meetings – Coaching principles can be applied in a team setting too. A simple example would be to problem solve by initially eliciting from the team a number of ideas about how to solve a problem, and to then open up a debate on the pros and cons of all the ideas that the team have inputted. This underlines that coaching is as much a philosophy and mind-set as it is a skill. Book 5. in this series, "Sales Management: Motivational Sales Meetings" provides ideas in a lot more detail about how to do this.

Influencing colleagues internally – Coaching principles can be applied very effectively to the influencing of others. It's absolutely true that people cannot be influenced... people influence themselves. This is why coaching is such an effective approach to influencing others. It's an approach which doesn't 'tell' others what to do, which is an approach which would more likely than not be met with resistance. Instead, asking coaching style questions challenges the other party to consider what the most effective way forward is going to be. This does not mean to suggest that influencing others requires the initiation of a full and in-depth coaching conversation, but rather that it's possible to use the key principles of questions during the conversation to influence... so asking questions to provoke thought, and enabling the other party to reach their own conclusion.

Take, for example, a Sales Manager who wants a colleague from the IT team to help train the sales team to use a new application of some description properly, and let's assume the IT team is under a lot of pressure and have intimated that they can only provide support for the time being on an 'absolute need to' basis. If the Sales Manager simply calls and states their 'want', then the desired support may not be provided. In fact, it probably *won't* be provided! A different approach would be for the Sales Manager to initiate a conversation something like: "*I've been thinking about how we can best help your work flows with things being as busy as they are right now. As you know, the team are being provided this new application, and it does require some training. I can certainly do some, but I'm wondering what would be the most time effective way of utilising your expertise. We could simply leave everyone to contact you individually on an ad hoc basis, or have you join us initially for just a short while to answer as many questions as we can 'up front'. What do you feel would work best for you? Or do you see any other ways we can do this?*" Other questions like "*…and how much impact is that likely to have on your time?*" would work too.

There's no reason why the Sales Manager can't provide some thoughts and input too, as this is a conversation rather than a pure coaching situation. The point is though, that the more effective influencing strategy is to adopt a style during the conversation which is more of a coaching style rather than a telling / direction style.

Key thought: coaching principles can be applied to influencing others, both internally and outside of the organisation.

Influencing external partners (distributors, resellers, etc.) – and exactly the same approach works well with external partners too. Positioning yourself as a helpful 'sounding board' who supports problem solving certainly enhances such relationships. For example, should a reseller want advice on how to promote a product to a particular account, it's absolutely true that it's the salesperson of the product rather than the reseller who's the expert on the product, but it's also absolutely true that the reseller is the expert on that particular account. So asking questions like… "*What key goals does this account have right now? What features of the product will most effectively support them in the attainment of these goals? Who else involved in the decision making process needs to be impressed by your proposition? What other internal barriers within the account could slow down or prevent the purchase happening?*", etc., will help the external partner think things through so they come to their own rational conclusion regarding what the best steps to take are going to be.

Don't be surprised if at the end of a conversation like this you hear the other party say "*Thank you. You've been really helpful there!*" – even when you've inputted little or even nothing at all. You have been helpful – not by telling, but by helping them to think about things. And as with the example above, it could well be appropriate to add in an occasional comment and extra relevant piece of information. That's fine of course, it's what a conversation is all about. Helping them to reach their own conclusions though is teamwork.

When consultative selling – It might well have become apparent from the above two examples that there are a lot of parallels between coaching and consultative selling. Both are based on the use of effective questioning and listening skills, and both are approaches which aim to help the customer reach their own conclusions by helping them to think things through logically. Both help the other party to influence themselves!

Before and after the sales team attend development events – More detail about this in chapter 4. Suffice to say here that doing this effectively has a massive impact on ROI from participation in development events.

Field based coaching – a very big and important area in its own right. So much so that Book 4 of this series is dedicated to just this topic.

Pretty well anytime! – Coaching is a lot more than just the structured GROW model (or indeed any other coaching model) of asking questions. This is about the Sales Manager adopting the philosophical approach of their role being to…

- …draw the best out of their sales team.

- …treat the salespeople in the team as responsible adults and professionals, who given the right support, have the capacity to arrive at the right decisions for themselves.

- …bolster the confidence of salespeople by showing them that they can think things through for themselves, and can arrive at the right decisions.

- …lead and unleash the capabilities of everyone in the team in order to move the sales team towards both the longer-term Vision and achievement of shorter-term objectives.

- …develop a **culture** where everyone is constantly reviewing, learning, and planning for future success.

It might well be a lot easier to 'tell', and this approach initially might be less time consuming. But that's what the more **un**successful Sales Managers do. That's why it's so easy to make the following unequivocal recommendation:

Adoption of a coaching approach to managing individual salespeople and the sales team as a whole should be the standard and routine approach.

There are some circumstances where coaching is inappropriate (as already discussed). And in Book 6. of this series consideration is given to how style of coaching can be adapted depending on the specific needs of the individual being coached. For the most part though my unequivocal recommendation remains simple and to the point: **Coach!**

Introducing coaching to the sales team

For Sales Managers who've not previously adopted a consistent coaching style of management, putting into practice the ideas and principles this chapter describes may mean significant change, and change that's sufficiently significant for the sales team to notice a difference. This is certainly likely to be the case if coaching skills are being used for the first time following attendance of a coaching skills focused training course. In these circumstances the sales team will know in advance that the Sales Manager is going to attend a training course, and will be waiting and watching to see if they can identify any differences in what they do afterwards. Indeed, the more experienced (and cynical!) members of the sales team may expect there to be some differences, but may well have the attitude that "...*I've seen it all before... a manager goes on a course, and comes back full of new ideas that they try to put into practice, which in the fullness of time will disappear! So I'd best just keep my head down for a little while, make sure I don't get too close to them, and in a short time we'll be back to normal….!"*

This kind of attitude means two things:
1) The sales team will be wary of any new ideas or approaches the Sales Manager tries to take, and…
2) The Sales Manager will be wary of implementing any new ideas or approaches because they don't want to upset the sales team or to show themselves up!

For any training and development event or course, it's always important to not only develop a Plan of Action so what's learned is put into practice, but to also identify potential barriers to success and think through what solutions can be put in place to proactively manage them so the new ideas can be put into practice effectively. Implementing ideas about coaching having read this brief exploration of the subject is no different.

The first piece of guidance I'd offer is: Don't try to implement too many ideas too quickly. Initially aim to try out one or two simple ideas to begin with. Introduce them conversationally, so in a manner which the person you're speaking with won't even notice as being any 'different'. But just because you try initially just one or two small things, don't think that the right ideas implemented in the right way won't all the same make a difference.

A good example of this was a European Sales Manager who part way through a course I was facilitating which included the topic of 'coaching skills', had a telephone conversation with his account manager who was based in Italy. This call was to find out whether he had or had not won a new piece of business he was pursuing. The good news was that he had indeed won it. Not surprisingly, the Sales Manager was very pleased, and very happily passed on his congratulations. He also though tried out something we'd been discussing during the day related to coaching – positive reinforcement of positive behaviours. So he also asked questions like…

"…*so what did you do differently?*"

"…*what made you decide to do it that way?*"

"…*what alternative ways did you consider?*"

"…*why do you think that made the difference?*"

"…*what feedback have you received from the customer about why they chose us?*"

"…*where else could you apply these ideas you've developed?*"

"…*how are you feeling now about it?!*"

Simply listing these questions might make it sound like the style of the telephone call was an interrogation… which it wasn't of course… it was a conversation, and these are just examples of some of the things that were asked *during* that conversation. The point was that the Sales Manager was tentatively trying to apply two key principles of coaching: Coaching to reinforce success, and asking questions about what the salesperson did – the Inputs – so they recognised what they had done well and so could do the same things more consciously in the future.

The manager concerned told me and the rest of the delegates about what had happened over dinner not long afterwards. It was the result of the conversation that the rather animated and motivated manager described that was particularly interesting. He told us how this Italian account manager was quite mature, certainly experienced, and someone who wasn't often prone to emotion. And that the more questions the Sales Manager asked this person, the more animated, enthusiastic and emotional he became. At the end of the call, to quote the Sales Manager… "*he was almost in tears!*"

It was also interesting to note the Sales Manager's response to what had happened during the telephone call. He was astounded at how powerful simply asking a few simple questions had been. And made to the Group a really important point when he asked the rhetorical question: "*Why haven't I done this before…?*"

As I say, you don't need to make massive change to achieve massive impact.

The second tactic to use when introducing ideas and principles of coaching is to apply them to a simple scenario rather than a challenging and complicated one. The above example illustrates this well. The manager simply added into what was already a very positive telephone conversation just a few questions to encourage the account manager to talk through what they'd done. Trying out new skills for the first time in a difficult and tricky situation is never easy. And if things don't go well, it may mean that the situation isn't resolved as well as it otherwise would have been, and this in turn may discourage the Sales Manager from applying the skills again in the future. Taking on something difficult for a first try simply doesn't make sense!

> **Key thought: The best way to begin to utilise any new skill is to begin slowly and in easy to manage situations. This is certainly true of coaching.**

Another good tactic to use is to ask for the help and support of a recognised senior member of the team who you enjoy a good working relationship with.

Share with this person what coaching really is (and in particular explain the differences between coaching and directing!), what it entails, and the benefits to the coachee. Be honest and open about your desire to begin to implement coaching skills, and that you are aware that like any time when a skill is initially implemented, you're likely to be not as elegant a coach as someone more experienced with coaching. And then ask for their help as you engage on the journey, using coaching *together* to improve the quality of their Inputs.

Your colleague can then help and support you as you develop and hone your new skills. Moreover, when the rest of the team see that you're adopting this new approach with one of the more senior (and more likely than not more successful) members of the team, this will communicate that coaching is about helping and supporting <u>everyone</u> in the team, it's not just about addressing under-performance. I know of many Sales Managers who've taken exactly this approach, and found that it works really well.

Summary

Coaching provides an impressive list of potential benefits – to the salesperson, the Sales Manager, and the organisation as a whole. The simple fact of life is that objective studies have demonstrated time and time again, that the Sales Management teams in the more successful organisations invest more of their precious time to coach, and are more skilled at implementing this approach.

Coaching is the art of asking questions in order to help the person who is being coached (the coachee) think things through for themselves. The approach can be described as 'drawing out', which is very different to 'putting in', which is what training does. It is very different from 'directing' or 'telling', the biggest downside of which is illustrated by the use of sat navs – it prevents people from learning. Whether the Sales Manager adopts routinely a coaching or directing style of management will have a significant impact on the culture of the business.

Feedback is a means of providing the recipient with objective information about the behaviours they are using and/or the impact these behaviours are having on themselves and/or others. Objectivity is the key issue, and feedback can be used to inform the 'review' stage of the learning cycle if the coachee is lacking relevant and important information.

For Sales Managers who are embracing coaching for the first time, it needs to be realised that adopting the skill is not necessarily easy; it's very different to the skills involved in persuading the other party in a conversation to arrive at a pre-determined point, as is often the approach taken in a selling situation. There is no pre-determined point, other than a recognition that there is going to be an agreement regarding what Actions the coachee is going to take as a consequence of the conversation. Like any skill, it's not possible to learn how to coach, and to enhance and refine coaching skills by reading a book. It requires practice, practice, practice…

The GROW model which was first described in John Whitmore's book "Coaching for Success"(12) provides an easy-to-use structure when coaching. It doesn't have to be used in a strictly linear fashion, and is a structure which the coach can adapt to their own style and personality. When coaching, it's good practice to help the coachee arrive at their own conclusions by helping them to focus in on the consequences of their behaviours.

The approach and style that's adopted when coaching can be modified in order to fit the needs and requirements of the less experienced in the team. In particular, it's not a bad idea to ensure there's plenty of focus on positively reinforcing positive behaviours, very much a case of what my manager told me when I moved into my first sales training role: "*Catch them doing it right… Praise Pays!*" Although this is not a bad approach to adopt on most occasions with *everyone* in the sales team.

The coaching style the Sales Manager adopts can also be influenced by cultural issues and the personality of the individual being coached. This requires quite advanced skills, and underlines just how big the subject of 'coaching' really is.

It's important for any sales team to have recognised standards which describe 'best practice'. The National Occupational Standards in Sales are a resource which can help organisations develop such standards if they are not already in place.

There are times when coaching is inappropriate and a 'tell' or more directive approach is the more appropriate style to adopt. These include to ensure legislation is adhered to, when the consequences of failure are unacceptable, training is required (so 'putting in' is required), and when addressing unacceptable behaviours in the workplace. For the vast majority of the time though, coaching should be the preferred way forward.

For Sales Managers who this chapter enthuses to embrace coaching for the first time, then the guidance provided is to begin slowly and steadily, and to utilise coaching to address relatively simple situations to begin with, and with the people in the sales team who are the easiest to converse with. Indeed, it might even be useful to proactively, and very openly, enlist the

127

help and support of an experienced peer leader within the team; that would send out a clear message that coaching is about helping and supporting everyone in the team, and is not just about addressing under-performance.

For all Sales Managers though, the recommendation is unequivocal: **Coach!**

4. Maximising Returns from Training & Development

The amount of cash resource that's spent on 'Training & Development' is colossal. The total spend in the UK during 2013 is estimated at having been £42.9 billion, which equates to £2,550 on average for every UK employee(14). And of course the *real* cost of training is a lot more than simply the cost of the course, or e-learning materials, or whatever the money has been spent on. Time that the sales team is taken away from its core purpose of selling equates to lost sales ('lost opportunity time'), and at fear of stating the obvious this does not help the Sales Manager achieve their job purpose of *achieving sales through others*. For field based teams there may well be travel costs plus budget required for overnight accommodation.

> **Key thought: Time is arguably more valuable than money and budget. Achieving more sales can replace money and budget that's been spent. But once a day is gone, it's gone forever. It's irreplaceable. And that's why time is arguably more valuable.**

Now all this certainly doesn't aim to develop an argument that resources should not be invested in Training & Developing the sales team. It is meant though to provoke thought about what training really costs – which is significant. Moreover, it's meant to suggest – very strongly – that resources invested in training should be exactly that – an investment – and an investment that achieves a healthy and impressive Return on Investment (ROI). What should be avoided is a 'spend', which is what happens when budget, time, and other precious resources are allocated to Training & Development, and this spend either fails to achieve healthy returns, or even any returns at all; the words 'spend' and 'investment' represent different things.

I've spoken on a few occasions at Regional meetings of the Chartered Institute of Personnel & Development (cipd) on the subject of 'training effectiveness', and often start the presentation with a quiz to gain early participation and so win people's interest and attention.   The first question I ask is about the numbers above… the amount of money that's spent on training and development in the UK. Most of the audience are quite surprised at how much they under-estimate the answer. The second question I ask is this: "*The cipd has conducted research to estimate how much of this spend is wasted, i.e. fails to achieve its objectives. What percentage do you think this is?*" You may or may not be surprised that I'm never given a number lower than 50%. Now I'm actually being rather mischievous asking this question, as I'm not aware of any such research that the cipd has conducted, and I don't know what the real answer is. But that's not the point. The point I'm making is: If we all believe that a minimum of 50% of precious training budget resource is being used ineffectively, why on earth aren't we doing more about it?!

Maximising returns from Training & Development is an enormous subject. Indeed, the subject is so big that seminars, conferences, training courses(!), and indeed formal qualifications devoted solely to the subject are available for full time Training & Development professionals, and all those who have a passion for this subject. Such an in-depth level of knowledge and expertise is not needed by Sales

Managers. None the less, it is important that Sales Managers have a clear understanding of the key issues which underpin training effectiveness and how to influence them. The aim of this chapter is to provide precisely this know-how.

Be clear on how to measure 'success'

When first engaging with organisations, I'm sometimes asked if we can guarantee that our training courses will achieve impressive results. Now this might seem like a simple enough question, but there is actually more to the question than there might at first appear to be...

(we'll return to the actual answer to this question later...)

Firstly, there has to be clarity about what's meant by 'impressive results'. A generic, simple, and clear way of identifying whether or not 'impressive results' have indeed been achieved, is provided by the Kirkpatrick model of learning evaluation(15). This model proposes that there are four different 'levels' of evaluation as illustrated in figure 13. This model can be applied not only to training courses, but to any and every development activity (e-learning, conferences, etc.)

The first of these levels is 'Reaction', which is about measuring how favourably delegates have reacted to the training. For training courses and training workshops, this is normally achieved via the completion of a paper based or on-line evaluation form when the event finishes, or sometimes the morning immediately afterwards. Or it could be about the Sales Manager asking one of the team what they thought about the content of a seminar or conference they've attended. So level 1 evaluation is all about measuring the perceptions of the person who's attended.

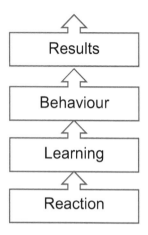

figure 13. The Kirkpatrick model of learning evaluation

There are some benefits to doing this. If the sales team has attended a training course and everyone who attended rated the content and delivery of the course as being 'poor', then it's important that the Sales Manager is alerted to this situation as early as possible. One would hope that the provider of the training event would want to provide this early feedback too, be they an internal training resource or external consultancy. If the evaluation form that delegates complete provides the opportunity for them to make comments, as well as rate specific issues against a numerical scale, then this subjective feedback can be useful too.

There are though very significant drawbacks if this is the *only* way that training effectiveness is measured. Firstly, just because participants have had a good time and enjoyed the experience, it doesn't automatically mean that the investment is going to provide any tangible difference to sales Outputs. It just means that the participants think the training has been 'good' – though what exactly 'good' means depends on how the questions on the evaluation form were phrased in the first place!

When organisations measure training effectiveness in this way, then they are also measuring the effectiveness of the training professional who facilitated the event in this way. If the training professional concerned wants the sponsoring manager(s) to rate them as 'highly effective', then they will naturally do what they can to ensure that the scores delegates put on the evaluation forms are favourable – which might mean a bias towards ensuring delegates enjoy a motivational experience rather than necessarily an effective development experience. Now these two things are not mutually exclusive of course; indeed, it is important that delegates do feel enthusiastic (and even excited!) about implementing what they've learned. But, the danger can be that either consciously or sub-consciously, the over-riding drive will be to ensure that delegates say positive things about the event (and in particular the trainer) at its conclusion. This is particularly true if an external training consultancy is being used, their effectiveness is being measured in this way, and further future business opportunities (income!) are going to be based on how 'effective' the event they've provided is believed to have been. Little wonder that in the sales training industry the evaluation forms that are completed by delegates on conclusion of a development event are referred to as 'happy sheets'!

Worse still is the message that consistent use of only level 1 evaluations communicates to the sales team: "Training effectiveness is about if you liked the course". No it's not. It's about the ROI in terms of increasing the quality of the Inputs, in order to increase the quantity and/or quality of the Outputs, as we'll discuss when considering level 3 and level 4 evaluations.

Key thought: 'Happy sheets' provide only a measure of effectiveness at Kirkpatrick's Level 1 (though they do have some benefits including an early alert if something has gone wrong).

Level 2 learning evaluations focus on the degree to which the "intended knowledge, skills, attitudes, confidence and commitment" have been acquired… so is about measuring the difference in what attendees *can do* because of their attendance of the development event. For a salesperson who's attended a training course which provides presentation skills, this would be about them demonstrating their ability to implement the skills the course provided to specific standards. Or for a salesperson who's been completing an e-based course about competitors, measuring their ability to recall key information such as the names of the top 5 competitors, the strengths and weaknesses of these competitors, and the key arguments that support selling against them successfully.

Level 2 learning evaluation is clearly more meaningful than level 1. The difference between the two can be illustrated by applying these two potential ways of measuring training effectiveness to measuring the effectiveness of a swimming lesson. A level 1 approach would entail finding out if the participants thought the lesson was 'good', and a level 2 approach would entail asking them to swim from one end of a swimming pool to another in order to demonstrate that they can utilise the skills the course has provided.

When employed in the pharmaceutical industry in the early part of my career, the induction programme and initial training programme was in-depth and intense, and lasted if I remember correctly around six weeks. Part of the training involved learning about the products I was to promote, and this was achieved by me reviewing learning materials at home (a 'Product Pack' which contained all the information about the product, its uses, its competition, etc.), followed by time at head office to learn more in depth information about the products and the disease entities they treated from the medical department. On the first morning at head office, the very first thing I had to do was to complete a written exam about the information I'd learned. There were no hidden agendas here by the way... It was stated in the Product Pack what the questions in the exam were going to be, and the answers that I was expected to provide. What was being measured was my *recall* of the key information – a level 2 evaluation. Once I'd achieved the required pass mark (90% or more), I'd commence work on rehearsing and practicing applying this knowledge in a sales situation. I was required to demonstrate that I was able to achieve specific levels of quality via role-plays before I was deemed to have completed the course – another level 2 evaluation of learning. Interestingly, I can't recall ever completing a happy sheet (though this was a rather long time ago!)

Level 3 learning evaluation is about measuring application of the same skills, knowledge, and know-how in the real world. So for a salesperson who's attended a course on consultative selling skills this would be about them structuring the face-to-face sales meeting effectively, using questioning and listening skills, etc. during a real sales meeting with a real customer. There can sometimes be a big difference

135

between delegates demonstrating ability on a training course, and then doing the same thing in real life. When I was first learning how to sell pharmaceutical products, this was achieved by my Regional Sales Manager observing me conducting sales calls with doctors.

> **Key thought: There is a difference between information that needs to be recalled without prompting, and that which needs to be understood and the salesperson simply needs to know where to access this information when required. Don't be shy about measuring recall of the former...**

And finally, provided that what's been learned is being utilised fully and effectively, then there should be some measurable impact on the business. Measuring this impact is a level 4 evaluation. So for the salesperson who's attended the course on consultative selling skills, this is about measuring the change in objective measures such as conversion ratios, average value of sale, and overall sales Outputs.

Justifying investment

As mentioned earlier, 'investment' in development activities involves more than just cash resource, but also time and other critical and finite resources too. The most effective means of justifying this investment is to measure effectiveness of Training & Development activities whenever possible at level 3, and preferably also at level 4.

Sales Managers who do this…

- …send a clear message to the sales team of their expectations that what's learned will be implemented, and that better quality and/or increased quantity of Outputs will be achieved as a consequence.

- …send a clear message to the training professionals who will be engaged with the sales team that there is an expectation that delegates will be able to apply what they've learned, and that the skills and/or knowledge and/or attitude that's being provided will impact positively on Outputs.

- …provide a robust business case for investment in Training & Development activities, which in turn means that this investment is more likely to be supported by key stakeholders such as the Sales Director, Finance Director, and even Managing Director.

- …position themselves as a business focussed leaders who understand how to effectively grow the sales team.

- …differentiate themselves from Sales Managers who don't do this!

> **Key thought: When a high ROI is achieved from sales training, you don't need a training budget… the training will pay for itself!**

Sadly, my experience shows that far too many sales organisations use only level 1 evaluations to measure how effective training has been. Is it little wonder then that when trading conditions are difficult and as cash resources become sparse, one of the first budgets to be cut is the training budget?

And there's absolutely no logic to this whatsoever of course. Imagine for a moment a football team that's found out that the forthcoming playing season is going to be tougher than it's ever been before, and the competition even more aggressive and fierce. Can you imagine the coach announcing: "*Right team, in response to this I've taken the decision that we're going to stop training.*" Or indeed can you imagine an army preparing for a battle that's going to be tougher and more competitive than ever before and deciding that the best preparation they can do is to stop training?!

However, there's another argument that makes this decision very logical: If plenty of cash resource has been spent on training in the past, and there is no objective evidence of ROI (so there is no evidence to show it wasn't a 'spend' rather than an 'investment'), then it makes sense to question whether the sparse cash resource should be spent in the same way again. Particularly if it can be allocated to other activities that provide a proven and healthy ROI when returns are now even more critical than before.

It's clear then that part of the responsibility that Sales Managers have, is to ensure that whenever possible, the returns accrued from development activities **are** measured objectively. That doesn't necessarily mean that it's the Sales Manager who has to *do* this though. Management is about *achieving through others*, and it may be that there is internal Training & Development and/or HR resource who can be asked to help. The same is true of course when using external consultancy support to develop the skills of the sales team; indeed, a quality consultancy should have a hunger and desire to do this, and be encouraging the Sales Manager to do so anyway.

Key thought: Consistent measurement of training effectiveness at level 4 brands a training function as a profit centre – very different to consistent measurement at level 1 which can lead to a branding of the function as a cost centre.

Another interesting issue related to justifying allocation of budget arises when some in the team fail to implement what they have learned. Let's consider two extremes: imagine two salespeople from the same team have attended the same development event. Assuming both developed similar Action Plans during the event, have similar levels of experience, enjoy similar tenure, and have similar sales responsibilities with similar challenges, then it would be reasonable to expect the investment in development to accrue similar returns from both of them. Imagine though that one of them has worked hard to implement their Action Plan, has overcome obstacles and challenges in the way, and as a consequence has evolved the selling behaviours learned from being initially strange and new ways of doing things, into highly effective selling habits. And as a consequence of this, there has been a significant increase in average order size. Imagine that the second salesperson though has invested practically no effort into implementing their Action Plan, selling behaviours haven't changed, and not surprisingly therefore, their average order value hasn't changed at all. What should the Sales Manager do?

The absolute correct answer here of course is "it depends..." as there could be many reasons behind the failure to implement the Action Plan, and it could be that there were other issues outside of the control of the second salesperson which impaired their ability to implement their Action Plan effectively, such as an emergency focus on the needs of a key account or maybe even a personal issue. But let's just imagine for a moment that they had as much opportunity to put things into practice as their colleague who has achieved notable success... what should the Sales Manager do?

Too often, the answer is to provide them with the same development opportunity over again in the hope that second time around they will do better. But where's the logic in this?

To provide an analogy... imagine for a moment you've trusted two financial advisors with £10,000 (each) to invest, and after 12 months you ask for an update on how much your investment has grown. Financial advisor No.1 has achieved a fantastic result, and even after their fees has managed to grow your investment to £12,000 – a 20% growth in just one 12-month period. Financial advisor No.2 can't even give you your original investment back, let alone give it back + extra achieved from growth. You now have a further £20,000 invest in the following year... how do you want to share this cash out?!

Investing more resource in a salesperson who has failed to implement what they've learned (and I must emphasise here, that we're assuming the situation is that they *could have* if they'd have wanted to) is rewarding negative behaviours. Meanwhile, failing to provide further training to the salesperson who has implemented what they've learned is punishing positive behaviours. It just doesn't make sense.

Now it must be emphasised here that salespeople need to be supported following development events, as we'll discuss below. However, sending a clear message to the sales team that... a) there is going to be a focus on level 3 and level 4 measurement, and that... b) achieving a healthy and impressive ROI from Training & Development is the salesperson's best way of gaining further investment in their skills and abilities, and so their future career – has a significant impact on culture. The culture should be one that invests significantly in meaningful Training & Development for the team, and one where the person invested in recognises their responsibilities in maximising returns from this investment. This is one of the key building blocks to what's referred to as a 'learning culture' within the organisation.

> **Key thought: An interesting question to ask might be:** "*If it was my personal money that was going to be used to pay for the Training & Development, how comfortable would I be that this was the right Training & Development, and how comfortable would I be that a robust process is in place which will maximise ROI from my money?*" **If you're not 100% comfortable, then perhaps something needs to be done to address this situation?!**

Maximising Level 4 returns

The Sales Manager has a responsibility to do what they can to maximise ROI from investment in Training & Development. In particular, they have a key role pre-briefing the team prior to participation in an event, and of enormous importance is how the Sales Manager follow-ups up and embeds what's learned afterwards. The critical importance of the latter was illustrated well by a study that followed two groups of

141

delegates who attended identical training events and whose management teams invested different amounts of effort to embed what was learned(16)…

The first Group attended the event and were simply asked to implement what they learned. They achieved an increase in productivity of 22.4% - pretty good; no doubt if a Sales Manager sent their team on a training course, left them to apply what they'd learned afterwards, and then achieved a 22.4% improvement in performance that would be a pleasing result! The second Group though, having experienced the same training event were also provided with "…*8 weeks of executive coaching, including goal setting, collaborative problem solving, practice feedback, supervisory involvement, evaluation of end-results and a public presentation*". This second Group achieved an increase in productivity of 88% - almost four times as much as that achieved by the first.

The message is extraordinarily clear – active and appropriate involvement by the line manager in the follow-up of development events has a **massive** impact on how much Outputs increase afterwards. This means that meeting with individuals who have attended a development event as soon as possible afterwards, and working with them to embed into every day practice what they have learned, is a high return activity, and so should be considered absolute priority.

If appropriate follow-up and coaching *does not* happen at all, then it's reasonable to expect (using the aforementioned figures) that there will be a 75% reduction in the Outputs which otherwise would have been achieved. Or to put this another way, if the Sales Manager makes an active decision to *not* follow-up when their team have attended a development event, then they are making an active decision to reduce the

ROI by 75%. Taking an active decision to reduce ROI by 75% is not easy to justify to the Sales Director, Board, or shareholders, let alone yourself.

It's also important to ensure delegates have a positive and open mind-set before participating in the development event, and have a clear focus on what's going to be gained from the event. So how the Sales Manager publicises the event, explains how it's going to be followed up and describes what their expectations are, are all important parts of the process.

What normally happens…

	The event	

↑ **Pre-brief**   ↑ **Follow-up & coaching**

What should happen…

Pre-brief	The event	Follow-up & coaching

figure 14. Relative importance of the 'before' and 'after'

So whilst the event is important (whether that be a training course, webinar, or anything else), the 'before' is actually an important part of the overall development process, and the follow-up and embedding is massively important. As illustrated in figure 14. though, all too often the amount of effort invested in the different parts of the process are not as 'right' as they should be.

So now is the time to return to that question from the beginning of this chapter: "Can we guarantee that our training courses will achieve impressive results?" Well, the training can provide impressive results in terms of delegates being able to do things differently afterwards. If they DO do these things, then yes, we would expect impressive (level 4) results. The overall effectiveness of the event though will be impacted on by how well the Sales Manager pre-briefs, and in particular on the follow-up coaching that delegates enjoy afterwards. So the question should not focus on just the training course... it should focus on the overall development initiative which includes the 'before' and 'after' as well as the development event in the middle. The effectiveness of the whole initiative will be influenced synergistically by <u>all</u> the parties who are going to be involved in the process. So the question should not be: "*will your training course achieve impressive results?*", rather "*What do we **all** need to do in order to ensure that impressive results are achieved from the initiative as a whole?*"

Key thought: As we state on the training events we facilitate... "Whilst the training event is important, it's what *happens* as a consequence of the training event that's <u>really</u> important!"

And though the discussion about responsibilities has focused latterly in this section on the provider of the training event and the Sales Manager, it's also true that the salesperson themselves has a responsibility to make the most of the development opportunity. Indeed, it's arguably true to say that the principle responsibility lies with them, with other parties inputting to help and support them along the way.

A recipe for success…

All the key points from the discussion so far can be used to inform and develop a simple, yet very effective process, that the Sales Manager can use to maximise ROI from all training & development related activities. Whilst the language used in the following description refers to 'development event', do note that this approach can be modified so that it works effectively for any and every development activity, be that a training course, e-learning, or even just the reading of a book. And to emphasise again, the mind-set should be one which focuses on the development initiative overall, just one part of which is the event itself.

1) Pre-brief: This initial meeting of minds between the salesperson and Sales Manager should provide clarity about what the initiative is going to achieve, how the initiative is going to be managed, and what the responsibilities of all parties are. The Sales Manager should adopt a coaching style for the conversation. If geography means that a face-to-face meeting can't happen (which is the preference), then the same meeting happens virtually.

It's recommended that a document similar to the one in figure 15. is used to guide the discussion. The first part of the document focuses on the business focused objectives – the Key Performance Indicators (KPIs) that the initiative aims to influence. This could include measures such as conversion ratios or amount of time between the first customer meeting and first order achieved in a new business selling scenario, or levels of customer satisfaction measured via quarterly surveys or average order value in a key account selling scenario. By helping the salesperson to focus on the Outputs the initiative is going to influence, a clear message is being communicated about the fact that development is not just about attending a course,

"Title of Development event"

Business Objectives

	Current Performance	Post workshop objective	+ 3 months
KPI (1)			
KPI (2)			
KPI (3)			
KPI (4)			

Action Plan

Potential barriers

Actions to manage barriers

figure 15. Documentation used to drive the development initiative watching a pre-recorded webinar or anything else – it's about enhancing business results. This also reinforces the expectations of the Sales Manager, and helps to build and embed a development culture within the sales team. Following a coaching approach, the Sales Manager is likely to explore…

- …what the perceived difficulties / challenges are related to improving each KPI.
- ...how the salesperson currently applies their skills in relation to these KPIs.
- …what skills / know-how gaps the salesperson perceives they currently have.
- …how they are going to manage themselves and others in order to gain the maximum from the actual development event.
- …what support the salesperson wants following the event, and in particular what coaching support is going to be provided.

The KPIs that the salesperson wants to influence need to be listed, along with the current levels of performance against each of these KPIs. There doesn't necessarily need to be four different KPI's (as illustrated) - one is fine; it all depends on what's relevant to this specific occasion and this specific development requirement. Realistically, there will be times when it's difficult, if not impossible, to identify precisely what KPIs are going to be influenced, even though it's clear that development in a particular skill area is relevant. All the same, *trying* to pin down KPIs with the salesperson does no harm in terms of reinforcing the culture.

Another benefit of engaging the salesperson in such a conversation beforehand, is that their mind begins to focus on what they need to look for – specifically for themselves and their own personal needs and requirements – during the event. This actually has an impact on how much useful information they 'see' whilst participating. It's rather like when you take delivery of a new car... all of a sudden there are thousands of the same make of car on the roads everywhere you look! And not surprisingly, you wonder where they've all come from! They have, of course, been there all the time. It's just that now you've begun to look for them, you've noticed that they are there. And that's exactly what the key content of development events can be like; once a delegate is tuned into noticing what's going to be important for them (by having been provoked to think about them in advance), then they are more likely to start noticing them.

> **Key thought: Think of those in your sales team who are participating in a Training & Development event of some description (training course, attending a seminar etc.) If an independent researcher contacted them by telephone and asked: "*Which of your KPIs are going to be influenced positively by this investment? And by how much?*" – what would they say?**

Also important is to schedule a follow-up meeting for as soon as possible after attendance of / participation in the development event.

2) The development event – Provides the actual *experience* required in order to develop the necessary skills and/or knowledge and/or attitude.

3) Debrief – Absolutely critical, and along with the follow-up coaching will have an enormous impact on effectiveness of the development initiative and ROI.

Adopting a coaching style, the responsibility of the Sales Manager is to help the salesperson to think through precisely what they are going **to do** differently as a consequence of the development event. If the development event has been a workshop of some description, the likelihood is that precisely what the salesperson is going to start doing / stop doing / do more of / do less of, will have already been recorded. In fact, if a clear Action Plan has not been developed during the training workshop then something has gone badly wrong! This Action Plan should be a description of the higher quality Inputs that the salesperson is going to employ, in order to drive higher quantity and/or quality of Outputs.

It's also worth exploring what barriers there might potentially be to successful implementation of the Action Plan. For example, having attended a training course related to use of social media, a salesperson might want to 'conduct more in-depth research of prospects' prior to a first meeting. Great idea – but conducting this research will require an investment of time, during what are undoubtedly busy days already. It's certainly worth highlighting 'time' as an issue, and then providing supportive coaching to help the salesperson think through how they are going to manage their time more effectively so the preparation they want to do, does indeed happen. Again, this is about helping them to define higher quality Inputs.

It's at this second meeting where targets can also be set for improvements in KPIs; these are the changes in KPIs that are going to happen as a consequence of implementing the Action Plan. It's recommended that the person who sets these targets is the salesperson. This can be achieved via coaching, and will mean that the salesperson has ownership of the objectives that are set. These objectives also provide the ability to measure ROI - objectively. Having a specific objective to achieve also provides the opportunity at

"Winning Appointments by telephone"
Business Objectives

	Current Performance	Post workshop objective	+ 3 months
No. calls made per week	23	32	
Speaks : appts	12:1	8:1	
No. appts won per week	2 ˎ	4	

Action Plan
* Apply qualification criteria developed during course before the call to increase the proportion of calls that are made to quality prospects.
* More pre-call research to ensure that opening statement is specific to individual prospect and value proposition is targeted specifically at their needs & requirements.
* Review LinkedIn – gain introduction from common contacts where-ever possible.
* Utilise call structure from course.
* Be more assertive managing concerns – using responses to main / common concerns developed during workshop.

Potential barriers
Time management!

Actions to manage barriers
* 9.00am-10.00am Monday, Tuesday & Wednesday to be allocated to appointment winning activities.
* Minimum 10 calls per session

figure 16. Example of completed documentation

future meetings to recognise achievement of the objective, and 'recognition' is of course a powerful motivator.

When two or more in the sales team have attended the same development event, this approach also allows the targeted change in KPIs to be specific to the abilities and experience of the individual salesperson. For an inexperienced salesperson change in a given KPI might be modest, though for them still represent a healthy challenge. For a more experienced salesperson meanwhile, change in a given KPI could be greater as they are better able to manage high challenge situations. It's even feasible that for a *very* high performing salesperson who is simply having to adapt to a changing market place, simply *retaining* current levels of performance by adapting Inputs to the changes in the environment could be a sufficiently stretching target. The point is, that the objectives set can be specific and appropriate for each individual salesperson, rather than be the same generic objectives for everyone who's attended.

The document that's produced could look something like the one in figure 16.

Also at this meeting, there needs to be discussion and agreement on how the Sales Manager is going to support achievement of this plan – so how often coaching is going to be provided, the nature of the coaching – where, how, etc.

4) Ongoing support and coaching - As discussed earlier, coaching, encouragement and support by the line manager has a massive impact on the effectiveness of development events and so the ROI that they achieve. An unequivocal recommendation therefore is that this one of the Sales Manager's priority activities.

151

5) Measuring Success - After an appropriate period of time, the Sales Manager meets with the salesperson to review what's been achieved as a consequence of implementing their Action Plan. This provides an opportunity to reinforce the changes in their Inputs, reinforce the benefits the salesperson has enjoyed as a consequence of doing this, and most importantly... help them to savour and enjoy their success! This is an opportunity for recognition.

If the new behaviours have become firmly embedded, it might also be an opportunity to revisit what was learned from the original development event, and to begin to work on other skill areas too. It's normally the case that so many ideas come from attendance of a training course, that it's simply not possible to implement all of them in one go; far more effective is to concentrate on just a few of them to begin with, add these ideas to the skill set, and once embedded and added to the skill set return to the original list and work on the next small number of ideas on the list.

Also appropriate at this point is to consider ROI from the investment that's been made – how healthy is this? And if it is healthy and impressive, then this is a good time to ensure that those responsible for allocating training budgets are aware of this, and so have a clear understanding that further allocation of training budget to your team is a good business investment. Doing this will certainly enhance the brand the Sales Manager enjoys too.

> **Key thought: Using a simple pro forma such as the example in figures 15. and 16. Is a lot more meaningful and professional than a 'happy sheet'!**

Team training initiatives

There will be occasions when the sales team as a whole participates in a development initiative, for example a bespoke training course focused on a specific aspect of selling skills. Exactly the same process as above can be adopted in these circumstances – indeed the opportunity for each person to set their own specific post-event objectives fits these circumstances particularly well.

What also works well in these situations is to arrange a follow-up meeting with the team as a whole after a period of time which has been sufficient for them to apply their Action Plans, and for them to have made an impact on the targeted KPIs. Moreover, as a key part of this meeting each person can provide their colleagues with a brief presentation outlining:

* The Action Plan developed as a consequence of the course (the Inputs).
* How well this has been implemented.
* What's been achieved as a consequence (the Outputs).
* What extra lessons have been learned along the way.
* Any challenges that have arisen that they want help with from their colleagues.

Adopting this approach provides an opportunity to recognise success - and for this to happen in front of peers and colleagues is an even more potent motivator than receiving recognition during a one-to-one meeting with the Sales Manager.

If this approach is to be taken though, it's important to signpost this right at the beginning of the initiative. If the meeting and the role that delegates were expected to take were a surprise, then this is likely to be perceived as quite threatening… "*…is this the Sales*

Manager trying to catch us out?"! Signposting it right at the beginning of the initiative though provides an opportunity to emphasise that this is about recognising and celebrating success, and for the team to share ideas and problem solve together. Now that's very positive! It certainly does though put some peer pressure on each person to actually <u>do</u> something with the Action Plan they develop, and if they experience positive outcomes as a consequence of doing this, then these actions will become self-reinforcing, which is no bad thing at all!

Again though, the key message is: Effective Training & Development is not just about the Training & Development event; it's about the entire initiative.

Some other thoughts…

With the focus of this chapter being 'Maximising Returns from Training & Development', here are a few more thoughts which will help achieve this…

Don't spend money on training courses if you don't have to – Remember the analogy in chapter 1. about the garage mechanic who could have just been provided with a laminated aid-memoire rather than being sent on training course after training course?! Always ask: "*Is there an easier / more cost effective way of achieving the same thing?*"

Invest wisely – Do consider the amount of returns that are going to be accrued and the size of investment required to accrue these returns. Is there a good balance in place? Admittedly, there is a degree of grey here rather than just black & white, as an appropriate and effective development event is also going to be an impact on levels of motivation and engagement, and there are times when the outcomes of Training & Development are not as easy to measure objectively as would be ideal in a 'text book' approach. Perhaps a good 'rule of thumb' would be to ask the question: "*How happy would I be justifying the decision to invest if stood in front of shareholders / the business owner / the Managing Director?*" If you're feeling comfortable with the answer to that question, then the likelihood is that the right decision is being made.

Beware the myths! – even today, there remain a lot of myths in professional selling, by which I mean statements of 'fact' that are accepted as being true, but in reality are actually not true at all. And when the person who's spoken the myth is challenged about the evidence or data to back-up what they've said is 'fact', they say something like: "… *don't you know… it's a well-known fact*"!

Here's an example: Did you know that a study by someone called Mehrabian showed that 55% of communication can be attributed to body language, 38% to tone of voice, and just 7% to the actual words that are used?

You've more than likely come across this 'fact' in conversation, on a training course of some description, or been told this during a presentation. In fact, it's simply not true. It's a myth.

Albert Mehrabian's work is discussed in his book "Silent Messages"(17) (along with work from many other investigators). He did indeed investigate the role of words, voice tone, and body language in communication, but the truth is...

- The work is focussed specifically on "*the resolution of inconsistent messages*", in other words, when someone is using words to communicate one message, but their body

155

language / tone of voice is expressing a different message.

- Albert Mehrabian himself states that his research was **never meant to be applied to normal communication**.
- The figures are based on amalgamated results of different experiments from different workers.
- A lot of the work is based on listeners interpreting individual words – not conversations or even individual sentences!

If 55% of communication really is down to body language, and a further 38% to tone of voice, then you'd understand 93% of what the locals are saying to you when you're on holiday abroad and you don't understand the local language that's being spoken! The reason you don't is because this simply **is not true**.

Now this is just one example of a myth, though it is probably one of the most widely held inaccurate beliefs there is in professional sales. It does though underline an important consideration when maximising returns from Training & Development: work with training specialists (internal or external) who have a full and deep understanding of the subject matter, and whose expertise is built on up to date knowledge, research, and facts... not myths!

There's more discussion about how to select an external partner in chapter 9.

Summary

There is a cost to Training & Development in terms of both training budget, and time. And time is arguably the most valuable resource of all. Whether the training budget can be said to have been 'spent', or 'invested', all depends on what happens as a consequence of its use. A healthy and impressive ROI means that it is most definitely an investment.

Measuring Training & Development effectiveness can be done in a number of ways, and the Kirkpatrick model(15) provides a straight-forward and clear description of the four different levels of measurement that exist. Whenever possible, effectiveness should be measured at levels 3 and 4. Indeed, in the sales discipline, this is relatively easy to achieve.

There is a process that Sales Managers can follow when managing investment in Training & Development. This entails ensuring mind-set is focused in advance of any event, and that there is robust follow-up afterwards which involves ongoing coaching and support. Focusing participants on effecting specific KPIs ensures the whole process is meaningful, provides a means to calculate ROI, provides an opportunity for recognition and to enhance motivation, and drives the development of a business focused learning culture. When managing the Training & Development process with the sales team as a whole, the opportunity exists to bring the team together subsequently to share successes, learn from each other, and celebrate successes.

We shouldn't be asking "*Is the training event going to be effective?*", we should be asking "*Is the training initiative going to be effective?*". The people responsible for this are the training provider (who could be internal, external, or indeed virtual), the Sales Manager, and principally the salesperson themselves.

When the Sales Manager manages the Training & Development process effectively, they have the means of demonstrating that Training & Development

157

is a profit creating activity rather than a budget spending activity, provide the financial arguments that support the winning of further Training & Development resource, and enhance their personal brand in the organisation. 'Training & Development' is not just about courses and workshops; it's about e-learning, reading, attending conferences, and indeed any activity that enables the person or team involved with skills, and/or knowledge. Applying a robust process to managing learning therefore should apply to *all* of the opportunities that exist.

5. Core development activities

It's important to stress again (and without apology!) that the term 'development' relates to developing not only skills and knowledge, but also 'attitude' - a rather intangible term that encompasses issues such as 'confidence', 'mind set' and 'enthusiasm'. Intangible these things might be; but aren't they important?

Also important is to reiterate that 'development' is not necessarily about a training course. Yes, a training course is one way of achieving development. But there again so is going about the day-to-day job and reviewing, learning, and planning from experience. And the support of a coach will expedite development in this situation of course.

'Development' might be about training, so the 'putting in' of skills and/or knowledge that wasn't there before. Equally though, it could be about reviewing and honing a skill which is once again needed because of (for example) changes in the market place – but hasn't been used for a while so is a little rusty. So a 'development event' of some description in these circumstances might be useful, and it probably would be referred to as 'training', though in the strict sense of the term this isn't really the case as it's more about 'drawing out' (again) than it is 'putting in'.

The purpose of this chapter is to provide some broad guidance on how to manage some of the main development activities that the sales team are involved with – whether the focus of this development is skills, knowledge or attitude, and whether they are designed to 'put in' new skills, or review and refresh what's already there.

Training courses and training workshops - overview

It's simply not possible to learn how to drive a car by reading about how do it... learning how to drive a car has to involve actually sitting in a car and driving it. That's because it's a skill, and the only way to learn a skill is to actually 'do' that skill. Training courses and workshops are development events which help to grow skills, but are, strictly speaking, slightly different to each other...

A 'training course' involves the provision of skills. So a newly appointed salesperson in their first ever selling role as part of their induction is likely to attend a training course on consultative selling, and so be taught how to sell consultatively. A 'training workshop' might involve similar input, but will also include work by attending delegates to *apply* the content to what they already know. An example here would be an experienced sales team who attend a training workshop where they are provided information about changes in legislation and how this is going to impact on customers in their market place, and then it's they who work out how this in turn should impact on how they sell.

In reality, the terms 'training course' and 'training workshop' have become intermixed. A lot of sales training providers like to use the term 'training workshop' to position a training course as an event which involves a great degree of participation and the delegates working things out for themselves (in a structured way). For simplicity, from henceforth the term 'training course' relates to both of these scenarios.

Training courses require an investment of time by those attending – which means lost selling time. So as well as the actual cost of the course, there's a need to take into account the cost of potential lost sales, and there might be travel, accommodation and subsistence too. More positively, courses encourage an exchange of ideas and learning between delegates, and team discussion can generate team solutions to issues. It's also true that those with an 'activist' learning style find this approach particularly stimulating (there's a lot more discussion on learning styles in "Sales Management: Motivational Sales Meetings", book 5. in this series).

Whether it be a course or a workshop, the broad guidelines about manging these events are similar, with the critical issue being follow-up and embedding of what's learned, as was discussed in some depth in the last chapter.

External v internal expertise

There are two broad options when it comes to designing and implementing a training course: Do it yourself ('yourself' being your company, and so includes utilising the expertise of colleagues such as the training team) or engage with an external consultancy. Which of these options is the most appropriate way forward depends on the circumstances, since there are pros and cons to both, as described in Table 5.

Similarly, when choosing to utilise external sales training expertise, there are broadly speaking two options again. The first of these is to simply book one or more delegates onto what's referred to as an 'open' course. This is a standard course that's scheduled to run on specific dates throughout the year. Anyone can attend these events, so participants will be from a

Internal expertise

Pro's	Cons
* Internal colleagues understand the specifics of the business. * Company owns the Intellectual Property (IP) of any developed ideas and materials. * No cost (to the Sales Manager). * Easy to liaise with colleagues in training on an ongoing basis. * No potential conflict of interest (i.e. internal colleagues not working with competitor organisations at the same time). * Can easily link course content into internal systems and processes (e.g. any internal TNA). * Easy to link together product and skills training (e.g. input from different company experts). * Materials branded with company logo – reinforces that this is "The company way". * Easy to utilise intranet and similar tools to follow-up and reinforce, and also to provide pre-course information. * Course can include content such as guest speakers from other departments (e.g. marketing)	* Trainers will not have acquired wider knowledge and expertise via interactions with other companies. * May be perceived by sales team as less credible than an external consultancy. * Sales team potentially always working with the same small number of trainers. * Internal trainers likely to be generalists rather than specialists. * Sales Manager may be cross-charged for the services of the internal training team.

External expertise	
Pro's	Cons
* Will have significant knowledge of what other companies and industries do – which can be used to inform course design and content. * Training consultant is likely to be a specialist in that specific area (rather than a generalist) * External consultancies acquire new business via introductions and recommendations – so are motivated to provide high quality support. * May have access to their own data from surveys and studies. This might also have resulted in development of leading-edge approaches / tools / sales process / sales technique. * May be willing to license a course to clients who use that course routinely. * Sales Manager doesn't incur any cross-charging (if that normally happens in the organisation).	* Cost – of both the design and the implementation. * Any active follow-up by the external consultancy will require further cash resource. * More difficult to liaise with (as not based at the same site). * Less familiar with internal processes and culture.

Table 5. Pros and Cons of utilising internal and external expertise

Open courses	
Pro's	Cons
* Provides an opportunity to interact with delegates from other companies & industries, learn from what they do, and also develop networking contacts. * 'Tried and tested' formula/design to the event. * The trainer will have facilitated the event on previous occasions and so knows how to derive maximum benefit from the event. * Experienced facilitator will have acquired 'real life' examples from other companies that have attended the same event in the past.	* May not be specific to the needs of the sales team. * Some of the content may not be relevant to the needs of the business. * Can't be tailored. * Scheduled to run on specific dates. * May be cancelled if there are insufficient delegates booked on the course. * Doesn't usually include any follow-up.

Bespoke courses	
Pro's	Cons
* Tailored very specifically to the needs of the business. * Will not include any irrelevant content. * Can include follow-up coaching and/or a formal follow-up event to allow delegates to share successes. * Can be provided (if necessary) in smaller instalments over a longer period of time rather than via just one large event. * Sales team can be actively involved in the design and/or delivery (enhanced buy-in). * Can include elements delivered by a number of different specialists (e.g. internal product expert alongside an external sales expert).	* Requires a number of people to attend (less than 4 delegates is likely to be more expensive than all of them attending an open event). * Cost of design. * May be implemented as a 'one off' and so not accrue economies of scale / repeats. * Untried and untested 'formula'. * No objective data related to effectiveness of event (in advance of its implementation).

Table 6. Pros and Cons of standard ('open') and bespoke training courses

variety of different organisations and indeed potentially a variety of different industries.

Alternatively, sales consultancies can provide bespoke support – so an event which is designed to the specific requirements of the client organisation. This might be based on a standard open event, or literally designed from scratch. The pros and cons of the two approaches of 'open' v 'bespoke' is summarised in Table 6.

The quality of bespoke events will depend on the quality of the consultancy utilised, and guidelines regarding selection of the appropriate partner in this instance is provided in Appendix 2.

It is, of course, standard practice to ask to speak to one or two satisfied customers when engaging an external consultancy to provide bespoke support. However, there is no reason why the same can't be done when deciding on which open course is going to be the best for a particular training requirement too. Or there's no reason why the Sales Manager can't ask to speak directly with the consultant who facilitates the course; in fact, a quality consultant in a quality organisation will actually welcome such enquiries as it shows that the sponsoring Sales Manager is taking the development of the sales team seriously.

So assuming that a training course of some description is an appropriate solution to the development needs of the sales team, the good news for the Sales Manager is that there are a number of options that can be considered. They do need to be considered though... there are pros and cons to all the alternatives, and what suits one situation doesn't necessarily suit another. The right solution is the one that best fits that particular set of circumstances.

Role-plays

Role-plays are a training activity, and normally take place during a training course rather than as a 'stand-alone' event. They're considered here though under a separate title because they are important – for two reasons...

First of all because when role-plays are conducted **in**appropriately, they are arguably the most effective way we've yet found to damage salesperson confidence and self-esteem! Sales Managers reading this will no doubt now be smiling, as they will have actually been in such circumstances themselves, or will know of colleagues who have – though I'd guess it's the former that's most likely!

The worst situation happens when some unfortunate soul is pulled out from a training course in front of their colleagues and forced to conduct a live role-play in front of their peers, with the person who's running the course role-playing the customer. We're all familiar I'm sure with the horror stories of how the person running the course in these circumstances wants to 'prove' they are the expert, and so conducts the role-play in an unrealistically difficult fashion. The salesperson role-playing feels under pressure and humiliated, and the audience feels embarrassed... although they probably feel rather relieved as well, because it's not them who have been chosen to be the one 'on stage'! Little wonder that role-plays have a bad reputation. What on earth is the point in conducting them in this way? If the goal of any development event is to enhance knowledge, skills and attitude, why conduct an exercise which is not going to help knowledge or skills, and is likely to negatively affect attitude?!

The second reason that role-plays are important is that when conducted *properly*, they are a **fabulously effective** means of increasing both skills and confidence. And from a logical perspective, they *should* be included in skills related training. It's difficult to imagine any profession that requires honed skills which *doesn't* rehearse the skills they are going to use in advance of doing them for real. Actors, musicians, surgeons, pilots, TV presenters and the police all practice the skills which enable them to perform their job properly. They rehearse in order that the Inputs they utilise day-to-day for real, are quality ones. It's very difficult to imagine the situation where a member of the London Philharmonic Orchestra will ever say: "*Don't worry about it… I don't need to rehearse …I'm sure I'll be OK on the night!*" Or even worse, a surgeon or pilot saying that! So why is it that this is what sales professionals sometime say? All too often we hear: "*Role-plays aren't realistic, and anyway, I'm sure I'll be OK once I'm in front of the customer.*" Why is this? Well, the answer is probably to do with the fact that the way role-plays are managed is normally dreadful.

It is not impossible for the sales team to find role-plays constructive, and to actually enjoy them (believe it or not!). And the more this is their experience, the more they will relish the opportunity to participate in them. Making them constructive and enjoyable is all about the way that that they are organised…

The first key issue is to ensure that those participating don't perceive the exercise to be a 'test' of any description. There are exceptions to this rule, the main one being when it's essential that a delegate needs to prove they can utilise a certain skill to specific standards before they are allowed to do the same things unsupervised. That's what a driving test is all about – the examiner needs to observe that the person being tested is able to utilise all the skills required in order to be deemed to be able to drive a vehicle safely and to given standards. When I was first employed as a training specialist, I wasn't allowed to coach trainees until I'd attended a 2-day training course on the subject, *and* had demonstrated to the satisfaction of the facilitator that I could implement the skills that I'd learned to a given standard. Then I was allowed to do it for real.

For the most part though, role-plays the sales team are involved with during training events are not going to be of this kind…they will be opportunities to rehearse and practice. With this in mind, why not call them this – rehearsals? Or even 'Rehearsal for Success'? As the saying goes, the label certainly then says what's in the tin!

Key thought: Why not brand role-plays as 'Rehearsals for Success'?

It should be emphasised from the outset by who-ever is running the course, that these exercises are not about proving that delegates can do it 'right', or 'better' than their colleagues – no matter how competitive a nature they have! It's about taking away from the exercise as many learning points as possible to inform their ability to increase the quality of their Inputs. The Sales Manager of one organisation I worked with helped with the coaching during the role-play exercise, and was absolutely delighted with one of the team in particular. Not because this salesperson did everything 'right' during the role-play, but because when reviewing the video of it afterwards, she independently identified everything that she could have done better, how she could have done these things better, and recorded on her Action Planning document precisely what she was going to differently day-to-day as a consequence of the review and

169

learning. This was a fabulous result, not only because of the constructive Action Plan the salesperson developed, but because of the professional way in which she approached the exercise in order to increase the quality of her Inputs. The Sales Manager was delighted because she had learned and grown.

As the actual role-play itself isn't (normally) a situation where proof needs to be provided of skills, then that role-playing time can be utilised by the delegate in a way which maximises the learning they achieve from the experience. That's why when briefing in a 'Rehearsal for Success' exercise, I include the rules:

- ⚬ "There are no prizes for 'doing it right'."
- ⚬ "There is no 'pass' or 'fail'. Though 'failure' could be considered to be: failing to gain ideas from the exercise."
- ⚬ "Be selfish – gain as much from the exercise and opportunity as you can."
- ⚬ "The exercise is not about conducting a perfect role-play – it's about using the opportunity to gain as many ideas as you can. So if part way through the conversation you think the question you've just asked wasn't worded properly then say '*Hang on – that was not what I wanted to say – let me re-word that question*'. If part way through the role-play you want to stop and think, then take a 'time-out'. If part way through you feel the conversation isn't moving in the direction you want, then feel comfy to say: '*Hang on – I think I'm taking the conversation in the wrong direction. Let's go back to an earlier point in the meeting and see if handling things in a different way works better*'."

...the more that the exercise can be set up so the salesperson takes ownership of the opportunity, and is given the opportunity to gain the most from the exercise, the better!

What works well in these circumstances is to ask delegates to work in Groups of 3 people, with one acting as the customer, a second acting as the salesperson, and the third as an observer who is there to support the debrief and discussion afterwards. The idea here is to conduct the exercise three times, so each person has the opportunity to take each of these three roles in turn. 'Being' the customer isn't just about helping the person role-playing and rehearsing for success. It's actually a useful learning experience in its own right... it can be very enlightening to experience the impact that selling behaviours (good and bad ones!) have on feelings and emotions, even in an artificial role-play situation.

Adopting this 'triad' approach to the role-play exercise also provides the opportunity to add on another rule to the ones listed above: "*If at any point the salesperson wants to take a 'time out' and discuss with the observing coach the best way forward, then that's fine too*".

> **Key thought: Using professional actors adds enormous value to *rehearsal for success* exercises. Indeed, there are companies which specialise in providing actors for corporate training events, and whose actors are also skilled coaches and facilitators.**

I knew we'd set up properly the 'Rehearsal for Success' session in the minds of a sales team I enjoyed working with recently, when one of the team described to me a specific customer that she had, and the concerns that she knew the customer was likely to raise during the conversation – and how she was going to brief the professional actor she was going to work with to voice exactly these concerns so she could rehearse managing them. Fantastic! This was a professional who had taken ownership of their personal development. And achieved a great result from the exercise I'm pleased to be able to say!

I'd engaged professional actors to help with the role-plays of this event by the way as it was critical we developed the mindset and confidence in delegates attending that they could manage customer concerns when introducing a change in pricing. And the best way to achieve that was to make the 'rehearsals for success' as realistic as possible – which is what our actors enabled us to achieve. Professional actors are not necessary or appropriate for every occasion; they are though a highly effective resource to use when the occasion is appropriate.

Video-recording role-plays

Powerful potent and effective… words that can be used to describe the use of video-equipment in conjunction with role-plays. Both positively and negatively! Again, it's all about *how* the equipment is used and the exercise is managed that's important.

It's critical first of all to be clear on the purpose of acquiring a video record of the behaviours that have been used during the role-play: it's to provide the salesperson with data which **they** can **review** in order to **learn** and as a consequence **plan** how to increase the quality of their Inputs on future occasions. The video record is not to prove they can do it right, or to provide the opportunity for the Sales Manager or anyone else to act as a policeman. The video-recorded material therefore should be 'owned' by the salesperson, not the Sales Manager.

The video material should be reviewed by the salesperson themselves, with the support of a coach. This may or may not be the Sales Manager. Following the principles of coaching, the review of the video-recorded interaction needs to include identification of positive consequences in order to identify the positive behaviours which elicited these responses – so they can be done in the future more consciously – as well as the less positive consequences, and the behaviours which elicited these responses – in order that they can be modified.

No matter what the facilitator says at the beginning of a course which includes video-recorded role-plays, and no matter how good the facilitator is at relaying the message that the exercise is not a test of any description, participants will all the same feel nervous. And this nervousness will increase when they walk into the room where the role-play is going to take place and see the video camera. To avoid this, try setting up the room as illustrated in figure 17.

This arrangement means that the video camera won't be seen by the salesperson when they walk into the room, and by the time they've sat down they'll be so engaged with their role-player and with the exercise that the camera simply won't affect what they are doing. In fact, on more than one occasion using exactly this set up I've had delegates ask after the exercise: "*Where did you hide the camera? I didn't see it at all!*"

This short section isn't about all the detail that can go into designing video-recorded role-play sessions; it's simply about providing an understanding of the key do's and don'ts. One last tip though: After they've completed their rehearsals for success, have two of the delegates review together each other's recordings. This will provide the opportunity to...

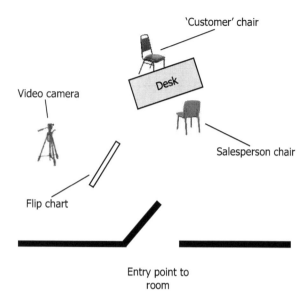

'Customer' chair

Video camera

Desk

Salesperson chair

Flip chart

Entry point to
room

figure 17. Room setting for video-recorded
Rehearsals for Success

- ...gain comments and critique from a colleague
  – who's thoughts are likely to be held in as high
  a regard as those of the Sales Manager (if not
  higher!).
- ...observe how a colleague manages the same
  role-play scenario, and probably acquire new
  ideas as a consequence.
- ...develop observational skills, and in particular
  those related to objectively observing selling
  and communication skills. These can then be
  used to 'self-coach' when the salesperson is
  working on their own.

Recording telephone-call based role-plays

Exactly the same principles apply to this scenario as to video-recorded role-plays (apart from positioning of the video camera!). Telephone recordings tend to be a lot shorter than video role-plays, which means that more practice opportunities can be provided over the course of a day or ½ day session.

There is also the opportunity for participants to apply what they've learned to real telephone calls with real customers. If this approach is adopted, I'd recommend strongly that there has been sufficient opportunity to practice and rehearse to ensure that these are going to be a success. Live calls should be principally about building self-esteem and confidence, rather than developing skills… very much a case of developing the mind set of 'I can'.

Having said that, there is clearly still a place for supportive coaching, either by the coach listening in to calls via a shared head-set, or by the coach reviewing a recording of the call. If this approach is taken, do ensure that local legislative requirements are satisfied (in the UK this would require a standardised verbal alert to customers that the call is being recorded, and inclusion of a similar alert on any marketing literature).

Sales conferences & sales seminars

These terms describe events where one or more speakers present to a large audience made up of attendees from different companies and industries. In this sort of setting, the learning is mostly passive; it's difficult for a speaker to be able to interact one-to-one with each of what could be hundreds of people in the audience. None-the less, a quality speaker will not just 'talk at' the audience, but also provide thinking time, and design their presentation so that delegates can interact with those around them in order to be able to debate and share ideas regarding how to apply the information provided to the specifics of their role and industry. Indeed, an opportunity to exchange ideas with fellow sales professionals from other industries can be very thought provoking and constructive. And of course such settings provide an opportunity to network and make new contacts.

There's an enormous variance in style and content of sales conferences. At one extreme of the spectrum are academic conferences which have robust content based on research, hard data, and facts, which is presented by appropriately qualified speakers. At the other extreme of the spectrum are 'motivational' sales conferences, where speakers are well known names and even celebrities, but whose content is not as robust as the former. There are pros and cons to each of course, and many conferences are a blend of these two approaches and so in the middle of this spectrum

Key thought: Sales conferences and seminars are of different style and their content is of differing quality. Select the events that best meet the goals you have for attending...

An example of the former would be the annual conference of the Global Sales Science Institute (GSSI), an organisation which aims to "...unite the study and practice of sales & sales management around the globe". Some sessions at the conference are focused on the presentation of new papers and research which is aimed at academia, and others are focused on leading-edge sales research and its applications to professional sales and so aimed at practitioners (such as Sales Managers). All sessions though are based on robust, researched, factually correct information. Conferences of the US based Strategic Account Management Association (SAMA) are similarly robust.

It's very dangerous to assume that the way customers purchase today is the same as it was even five years ago, let alone ten. The content of these conferences therefore is highly valuable, as it provides the sales profession with an up to date and robust understanding of what the more successful and less successful sales organisations and individual salespeople are doing *today*. At fear of stating the obvious, this is quite important information!

The content of presentations by motivational speakers on the other hand may or may not be based on robust research, and so might not be entirely accurate. I attended one such conference, and was rather intrigued by a percentage figure that was quoted on a slide by one of the speakers; I felt it was really quite important and powerful information. So in the Q&A session I asked for a reference to the research so I could read in more depth how this data had been acquired. The speaker had no idea where the percentage figure had come from. Not surprisingly, having found out that one part of the presentation was based on weak, if not imagined information, I automatically discarded *all* the information that this presenter had provided!

There is a recognised phenomenon (the 'hawthorne effect'), where if the event has provided 'hype' and been motivational, then delegates do afterwards achieve some elevation in performance. This elevation in performance though is due to 'hype' and excitement rather than substance, and so driven by an increase in energy rather than any significant change in the quality of Inputs. It's because of this that performance returns to the previous lower levels within around 3 months. Referring back here to the discussion in chapter 4. about 'happy sheets', this is another illustration of the difference between delegates providing feedback either on paper or electronically immediately after a development event that it's been 'good', and a development event having a sustained positive impact on Inputs - which in turn impacts positively on Outputs, and so is sustained in the longer term.

Key thought: Beware the hawthorne effect! Ensure the improved performance your team achieves via training is sustained, and not just a temporary 'shot in the arm' of motivation!

Now this discussion does not aim to suggest that the former more academic approach is right, and the more entertaining approach is wrong. Some in the sales team might find attending a more academic conference demotivating, but find the environment of a more relaxed conference more conducive to development. What the discussion means to suggest (and suggest strongly!) is that Sales Managers should think carefully about which conferences they do and do not use as development opportunities, which are indeed the most suitable for them and/or their teams, and which are going to provide a level of ROI that means that the ticket cost and attendance time is justified. If I were responsible for managing a very substantial global key account, then I would be very interested in attending a SAMA conference, and would probably be less inclined to attend a motivational event. If I were managing a sales team who had struggled through a very challenging period, were lacking vitality and would benefit from a proverbial 'shot of motivation', then I might make the opposite choice. It all depends.

Also bear in mind that some sales conferences are organised and chaired by sales consultancies, who are using the conference as a marketing vehicle for their company and/or the sales tool(s) they promote. That doesn't necessarily mean that the content is not going to be robust. In fact it's in the interest of the organising consultancy to ensure that the content *is* robust, as this will reflect positively on the brand of the organisation. It's reasonable though to exercise an approach of 'healthy questioning' in order to ensure the content is indeed the quality it should be. That's different by the way to 'unhealthy cynicism', which is a mind-set that begins with the premise that what's been presented is either misleading or untrue unless it's otherwise proven not to be the case!

One unique aspect of large scale conferences is the opportunity they provide to hear from eminent thought leaders. The cost of hiring a key global speaker to attend an event specific to your own organisation would be very high. Being one of an audience of hundreds though makes the cost of hearing them 'live' a lot more acceptable. But of course unless that speaker makes themselves available over a coffee break for one-to-one conversations (and then you have to be fortunate enough to be one of the audience who meets them!), there isn't the opportunity to interact with them in the same way as during a bespoke workshop. So there are pros and cons...

The Internet

To state that there's an enormous quantity of information about professional selling on the Internet is somewhat of an understatement! Many sales consultancies provide articles, blogs and video clips which can be viewed and/or downloaded for free, professional institutes do the same, and of course sales professionals produce their own blogs and videos too. With smartphones and the fast download speeds that are pretty well ubiquitous today, this means that this material can be accessed easily and whenever the viewer wants – so at home, during any 'down time' during the working day, and when travelling. If not viewed 'live', then material can often be downloaded for later consumption. Learning in small 'bit-sized' snippets is both time-effective and user-friendly; the learner can view what they want to, when they want to (sometimes today even when travelling on an aircraft!) And of course it can be accessed on a 'just in time' basis, as and when required.

Since anyone can upload anything onto the Internet though, the quality of this material varies enormously. Happily, much of it is decent and even good quality, and can even be based on objective data gained from research. The quality of some material though is questionable (and that is stating things diplomatically!).

Key thought: Beware the myths!

One thing to be conscious of when reviewing how robust the content of articles, papers, and presentations are, is that there is a big difference between a survey and a piece of research. A *survey* is a piece of research which asks for opinions. An on-line survey completed by salespeople who respond on a numerical scale between 1 and 5 to questions such as "*how skilled are you at listening?*" would be an example. A quality piece of *research* establishes facts rather than simply gains opinions. The research in Neil Rackham's landmark book 'SPIN Selling'⑩ is a good example. The research was carried out by professional observers who recorded what professional salespeople actually did during face-to-face meetings with customers (the Inputs), and in turn what customers did in response to what the salespeople did. The research was not a survey that asked salespeople what they believed they did in front of customers, and it did not ask customers what they believed they did in response to what salespeople did. The research established *facts*.

Two questions summarise what users of the Internet need to know when they are going to use this tool as a means of learning:

1) Where do I go to find the information that I want? And...
2) How do I know that the information is robust and so should be acted on?

Trusted networking Groups can be a useful source of guidance and advice, be they face-to-face (e.g. Sales Institute Regional networking Groups), or virtual (e.g. a Group on LinkedIn). But potentially this could mean each member of the sales team, or at best each Sales Manager within the business, finding this information independently – which in turn means a duplication of effort and inefficiency within the business.

> **Key thought: It doesn't make sense to re-invent the wheel! Is the training resource you need already out there somewhere?**

> **Key thought: Monthly Sales Tips are posted on the highcleresales channel of YouTube**
> **(https://www.youtube.com/user/highclere sales)**

Today, the likelihood is that what needs to be produced is already out there somewhere... it's just finding where that 'somewhere' is that's the challenge! It doesn't make sense for lots of different people to spend time doing the same thing over and over again by looking for the same resources. More sensible is for one person or function, as part of their role, to know where resources can be found, so that colleagues within the business can be provided with access to the resources which will provide the information required, and which are known to be robust and credible. That's why there's increasing discussion about the evolution of the training specialist within a business, from someone who creates materials to someone who has a knowledge of what resources are available and how they can be accessed. The term 'curator' is being used to describe this important part of the trainer's role today.

So for Sales Managers, a few questions you might want to consider are:

- Have you listed all the topics it would be useful for you and/or your team to have easy access to in order to learn, or to review & refresh learning completed in the past, and for which the likelihood is that there are resources on the Internet that would help?
- Has this list been shared with your colleagues in the training function?
- Does your organisation have a recognised methodology to create a list of relevant and

robust Internet based resources, and then to keep this list updated?

* Do you and your team make the most of such resources? And do you offer to coach the team in order to support their implementation of what they learn via the Internet?

Webinars

There are basically two different styles of webinar: Pre-recorded, where learners access and review the material at their leisure, or 'live' where the presenter is on-line at the same time as the learners and there is an opportunity to interact. Both have their place.

The content of pre-recorded webinars can be checked for both accuracy and how desirable the style of presentation has been before they are made available for viewing. So they should be materials of a decent quality.

Another positive aspect is that they can be accessed and viewed at a time and place that's most convenient for the learner – at home, during flights or rail travel, during evenings and weekends, etc. Moreover, once the material has been developed, it can be accessed over and over again, and can even be used as a reference tool by salespeople via hand-held devices, or for internal salespeople via an Intranet. Pre-recorded webinars though provide very limited scope for interaction, and this can impact on recall of information. They are really best suited to providing information rather than skill development, and because of the lack of interaction should ideally be no longer than around 45 minutes. In fact, *that's* quite a long time…

Live webinars overcome some of the drawbacks of pre-recorded webinars. Participants have the opportunity to interact with the presenter and ask questions, and the presenter can ask participants to complete tasks and exercises as part of the learning experience. If all the participants are based in one room together, then the presenter can even break the Group into smaller discussion groups, set tasks, and gain feedback – just as during a face-to-face training course. This approach is less flexible diary-wise though (as everyone needs to 'attend' at the same time), the content is less controlled, and the cost is higher, as the presenter needs to be there every time the webinar is provided rather than just on the one occasion it's recorded.

The science of creating and managing webinars is too large and in-depth a subject to be discussed in detail in this book; the simple point for Sales Managers to bear in mind is that today, this is another viable option to review when considering how to best develop the skills of the sales team.

Other e-learning

Over and above resources available via the Internet, there is of course an enormous array of other e-learning resources available. Some of these are standard 'off the shelf' products which help with requirements such as how to use CRM systems & databases, and how to use Microsoft software such as Excel. A really good buy of mine was a CD which taught me how to touch-type, though the trickiest bit was 'un-learning' how to type with just my index finger of course! Seriously though, ability to touch-type is a fundamental skill today, and so should be one that the

Sales Manager should help the sales team develop…
if they don't already have it, of course.

> **Key thought: how much time would be saved by each of the sales team and ideed the sales team as a whole, if they could touch-type?**

Others are bespoke and developed for the specific needs and requirements of individual sales teams and organisations by either internal or external expertise. More often than not, these involve 'gamification', which can help to initially engage users, and then keep them returning to the resource to use over and again.

Many of the comments related to the pros and cons of the Internet are just as true for e-learning… it can be accessed on a 'needs to' basis, used in short bite sized sessions etc. It's potentially less costly than a face-to-face training workshop, though that should be considered a bonus rather than a driving reason to select it. After all, the most expensive training is the one that doesn't do the job, so the cheapest money wise can be the most expensive when it comes to ROI.

Also bear in mind the comments in Chapter 1 regarding Generation Y: just because they're generally very comfy with technology, it doesn't automatically follow that their preference is to utilise e-learning resources.

Action Learning Sets

This is a term that's given to when a Group of people meet regularly to problem solve, subsequently take action, and to develop skills and knowledge as a consequence. Learning is achieved via a structured sharing of the know-how that's developed within the Group. This very often involves the support of a coach, or facilitator.

So this is not about formal learning... it's more about 'learning by doing', and then a sharing of that learning to maximise the benefits of it. The Group problem solving informs learning also. Principally though, this becomes an effective approach to growing people when there is a commitment 'up front' by all involved for this to happen.

Quite often Sales Managers do this in a less structured way via problem solving at team meetings, following-up action plans agreed, and then building on the experience again at subsequent team meetings. The question I'd pose for Sales Managers is: "*Can you do more to make this practical, problem-solving process more structured, and for your team to learn more via its implementation?*"

Summary

There are plenty of different ways that the Sales Manager can provide training for their team. *Which* is the best and most appropriate depends on the specific situation.

There is the traditional approach of providing a training workshop of some description, though even then, there are pros and cons to this being provided via internal or external expertise, and if via external expertise, whether it's a standard 'off the shelf' event of some description, or partly or totally bespoke and designed to address specific needs & requirements.

There are a lot of good reasons to include role-plays in skills focused training workshops; there is only one way you can develop and hone a skill, and that's by practice, practice, practice. It would be unthinkable for a professional in other industries to not practice, fine tune, and further develop their skills, surgeons being one such example! Why shouldn't professional salespeople be the same? Unfortunately, role-plays have been managed very badly over the years, and not surprisingly do carry with them now bad press and negativity. A few simple things can be done to make them an enriching and motivational experience though, not least of which is branding them as a '*rehearsal for success*'.

Technology, and in particular the Internet, has opened up a whole new world of development opportunities. Many high quality and helpful resources on the Internet are free. So are low quality ones though! It's important that the sales team is guided to relevant on-line resources which have robust content that's based on truth and hard facts rather than myths. All roles within a business are constantly evolving, and for the training specialist right now we're beginning to see more of a focus on their role as a curator of information and training resource, rather than the creator of it, at least not for 100% of the time. Sales Managers should be making demands now about the information they want their sales team to have access to…

6. Sales Qualifications, Training endorsements, and Professional Institutes

Sales qualifications – Introduction

For some reading this book, the idea of qualifications specifically for the sales profession might be a new concept; indeed, the very notion of formal sales qualifications *at all* might even at first seem a little strange.

Put into the context of other professions though, perhaps the idea that the sales profession is *not* more qualifications focussed should seem strange. Consider how you'd feel if you found that your doctor, surgeon, accountant or legal team were unqualified… and how would you then feel if when questioned about this they provided a response such as: "*Qualifications are for those who aren't 'naturals'! At the end of the day, it's not what you know but how well you can get on with the job that counts!*".

Hardly a response that would build confidence! So why do we accept that this is an acceptable state of affairs in the sales profession?

I've heard the argument: "*Yes, but sales is different to a surgeon or accountant where it's critical that those who are formally qualified know what best practice is, and have demonstrated their competence to the job*", And this is certainly an interesting argument. It suggests that for the sales professional, who is a

189

costly resource, who is being trusted by the customer to help them understand their problems and challenges and as a consequence make the most appropriate investment, and who is being trusted to represent the brand of the company they are employed by – knowledge of best practice and the demonstrated ability to do the job *are not* important! Of course, the very opposite of this is true.

Some would argue that the achievement of sales qualifications doesn't necessarily make somebody a good salesperson, and that's a fair comment. It's also true though that achieving a medical degree doesn't necessarily make someone a good doctor, or someone with a degree in accountancy a good accountant. It does though demonstrate that they have acquired, understand, and can apply the core information that underpins success in the role. Successful attainment of the qualification may well have required demonstration that they can utilise skills to a given standard too. This is the solid foundation onto which can be added all the other elements that contribute to sustained high performance, not least of which is continuing professional development (CPD).

It's also true to say that the challenges that face professional salespeople today (and this includes Sales Managers) are greater than ever before. Customer expectations are higher, competition more aggressive, intense, and agile, and the need to develop value-adding long-term relationships are now the norm rather than the exception. So arguably, attaining a solid foundation of knowledge and skills on which to build is more relevant now than ever.

The question could be asked: "*Well, why can't we just provide the same knowledge and skills via training rather than complete a formal qualification?*" And that's a good question. Any development activity should not be pursued simply because it's there – be it a training course, sales qualification or anything else, no matter how good the quality of it is. It should be pursued because it's the most appropriate way of achieving the development goals and so provide the skills, knowledge and attitude which are required to enable the sales team to exceed the sales plan. Having understood what knowledge and skills are required, the question then becomes: "*What's the best way to acquire these?*", and sales qualifications are one of the options which should be considered. They do provide some interesting and unique benefits though. Realistically, there are some drawbacks to them too.

> **Key thought: the challenges a professional salesperson faces today are arguably higher than ever before; it makes good sense therefore to ensure that they are more highly equipped with more skills, knowledge, and know-how than ever before - so they can successfully rise to these challenges.**

Sales qualifications – what they are

A sales qualification is an award which signifies that the student has demonstrated application of specific learning to a particular standard. So sales qualifications are not just about theory – they are about demonstrating both *understanding* and *application*. Depending on the nature and the level of the qualification, this can be achieved by…

- …the completion of written assignments which demonstrate application of knowledge and understanding to the specifics of the student's role and their business.

- ...the development of a portfolio of objective evidence which demonstrates application of knowledge and understanding to the specifics of the student's role and their business.
- ...recordings of role-plays and/or real interactions with customers (either face-to-face, or via telephone or other virtual media).
- ...live observations of role-plays and/or real interactions.

...or indeed a combination of these things.

All too often it's assumed that all qualifications are about simply remembering a lot of theory. This isn't surprising really, because for many Sales Managers this is what they remember from their time at school. This is not though what sales qualifications are about; they are acquired by the student **demonstrating application** of what they've learned.

So in order to gain a sales qualification, a student will indeed need to have knowledge. For someone working towards attainment of a qualification relevant to front-line sales, this would include elements such as 'what influences the customer's buying behaviour'. It's the demonstration of understanding and the successful application of this information that the student would gain credit for though, not just *having* the knowledge. For this specific example, this could be demonstrated by reviewing an actual customer, identifying what influences are relevant to their purchasing process, and then defining how this impacts on selling activity.

Key thought: Sales Qualifications are achieved by demonstrating *application* of what's learned – and not just by understanding theory!

So far from being theoretical, sales qualifications are in fact a very practical means of acquiring knowledge, and more importantly, of building skills and abilities.

Sales qualifications are available at a range of different levels, from a Basic award, through to Certificate, Advanced Certificate, Diploma, Degree, and Masters degree. Some sales professionals have even attained a PhD in a sales related area. In the UK, all qualifications are allocated a 'level' between 1 and 8, and sales qualifications are no different. So a certificate in sales will equate to either a level 2 or level 3 qualification, depending on the level of difficulty involved, and a Diploma in Sales to level 6 or 7. The key message for Sales Managers though is that appropriate sales qualifications are available for sales professionals in all roles, and for all levels of experience.

Benefits of sales qualifications

There are benefits to the salesperson who acquires the qualification, the organisation they work for, and of course the customers the salesperson interacts with.

For the salesperson, the obvious benefit is increased sales success! After all, the qualification is gained through *application* of know-how, not just acquiring it. When the qualification has provided the skills and knowledge that are known to drive success, and this know-how has been applied in the real world, then how can anything happen other than an enhancement of Outputs?!

Completing assignments develops report-writing skills; how to structure them, how to communicate clearly, and how to communicate with brevity. Indeed a student on one of the Diploma programmes I enjoyed the privilege of facilitating, was offered a promotion without any interview or selection process due mainly to the impressive quality and incisiveness of their Management reports. These skills had been developed as a direct result of having to write properly structured, high quality assignments, for each module of the Diploma, and receiving feedback and coaching so that the standards of these assignments constantly improved. The standards of his internal report writing had increased as a consequence too, and it was this that had been noticed and had led to his promotion.

Depending on the qualification, successful attainment allows use of designatory letters, DipS or Dip(Sales) for example (following attainment of a Diploma level qualification). Designatory letters certainly communicate a level of professionalism and enhance personal brand, particularly on business cards and e-mail sign-offs. They can also help to differentiate an individual from less qualified salespeople who work for the competition. And of course, those designatory letters can be used for the rest of a given individual's career, though this once again provokes a comparison to other professions... We take for granted that our doctor, accountant, solicitor, etc, invest time to retain up to date expertise and knowledge, and they don't just rely on what they originally learned at university. It's important that sales professionals do the same.

The discipline of having to invest time to study certainly develops the habit of reading regularly. At the very least, just one new idea picked up each week in this way adds up to a lot of new selling ideas every year. Retaining this discipline after the qualification has been completed will impact very positively on the individual's CPD.

Studying for sales qualifications provides superb opportunities for networking, both in the short and longer term. In the short term there's the immediate opportunity as part of the cohort they are studying with (assuming that the qualification is not being run 'in house' or virtually). In the longer term though, students can easily keep in touch with both those who were in the same cohort they were, and with others who have been, and are, studying also. In the UK, both the Chartered Institute of Marketing (CIM) and Institute of Sales Management (ISM) provide networking opportunities outside their sales qualifications programmes.

Key thought: The Association of Professional Sales (APS) in the UK at the time of this book going to press was in the process of launching a CPD system for professional salespeople. Refer to www.associationofprofessionalsales.com **for details.**

I argue very strongly though that the most significant benefit of studying for a sales qualification is the one that's most intangible: active and successful participation changes the way that the student *thinks*, and the higher the level of the qualification, the more that this is the case. At certificate level (depending on the focus of the qualification), this can mean a much more customer focused mind-set; once this is right, the skills, and know-how that the qualification provides fall into place very easily. It's a lot more difficult to embed skills and know-how when a less aligned mind-set is there. At Diploma level, students develop an enquiring mind, which questions everything and accepts nothing. Moreover, decisions come to be based on an objective assessment of all the relevant options available rather than simply based on what's been done before or the first idea or answer that comes to mind.

> **Key thought: The work required in order to acquire a sales qualification changes the way that you think.**

For the student's organisation (who will most often be their sponsor), the main benefit is the same as it is for the student themselves – more sales!   ...this increased quality and/or quantity of sales being derived from an increased quality of the student's professional sales Inputs, driven by application of learning from the qualification's curriculum.

Organisations which commit to sales qualifications communicate a clear message to their employees, their customers, and the market as a whole...

For employees, such a clear commitment to people development bolsters levels of motivation and engagement, both of which will have a positive impact – again – on sales Outputs.   Staff retention will increase too, not only because individuals need to remain with the organisation in order to complete their studies, but because...
1. ...the organisation has communicated clearly the message: "*our people are valued*", and
2. ...this is what happens as levels of engagement increase(18).

It also communicates with clarity the organisation's expectations regarding personal development and levels of professionalism that CPD is expected to maintain.   That impacts (positively) on both culture and the brand of the organisation.

To the market, a professionally qualified sales team communicates quality, professionalism and expertise. In a highly competitive world where purchasing organisations are seeking suppliers who can add value to their buying processes, this *must* help to differentiate and develop competitive advantage. Though it must be emphasised again, that it's not just having the qualification that matters, but applying the know-how the qualification provides in order to deliver Inputs of impressively high quality.

As the sales qualification focused organisation builds their reputation as a leading grower and developer of sales professionals, it becomes more attractive to potential employees. In particular, it will become more attractive to the higher quality candidates, who after all, will normally have a choice of which company job offer they want to accept. The better the quality of the material the Sales Manager has to work with as a talented leader, motivator and coach, the better the potential quality of the salesperson who they can help grow and develop in the longer term. Which again, has a positive impact on sales.

Attainment of a sales qualification can be used as an opportunity for recognition, and so a motivational opportunity too. Organisations which embrace sales qualifications quite often have the Awards presented by a senior member of staff such as the Sales Director or even Managing Director. Sometimes this is the key part of an Awards dinner or celebration, with photographs taken for publicity internally via newsletters and other similar vehicles. Such recognition again, sends out a clear signal to everyone in the organisation regarding expected behaviours and so the culture of the organisation (bearing in mind that again – it's important to send the message that it's the application of learning that's being praised, not just the completion of the learning).

And the purchasing customer enjoys benefits too – because they are dealing with sales professionals who are more highly skilled and customer focused, and who have a greater appreciation of the needs and requirements that customers have – because that's precisely the sort of know-how that sales qualifications provide.

It could be argued that the earlier references to sales qualifications leading to *more sales Outputs* is misleading; in fact what's happening is that the qualified sales team is better at helping the customer to buy… there's more buying going on and it's this that's driving the top line benefits to the sponsoring organisation.

There may well be some positive impact on customer emotions when they know they're dealing with a professionally qualified individual too.

With all these potential benefits, why is it that sales qualifications aren't the answer to all sales training needs? Well, because there are drawbacks too…

Drawbacks of sales qualifications

The most common argument that's put up against sales qualifications is they are too time consuming. And this is true, an investment of time is indeed required to gain the initial input, and to then demonstrate application of learning, which will very often be via completion of a written assignment. There is certainly a lot more to assignments than simply typing out a few pages on Word; the content needs to be thought through, researched, and often requires the completion of analyses before the content of the assignment itself is put together.

I personally have heard on more than one occasion: "*My job is very busy and it's difficult to find time to learn as well*". For those who have that attitude, I have some scary news... this IS the job! Expectations that what the most effective salespeople are doing today will be just as effective in 5 years' time are simply not realistic. Continual learning to evolve with, or more preferably to evolve in advance of, an ever-changing world, is what professionals do. CPD is not an option today... it's a necessity. More-over, development is not just about attending a course, it's about *applying* it afterwards, and the discipline of demonstrating application is an effective means of ensuring learning is indeed applied in the workplace. And to repeat a comment made above: developing strong report writing skills is important in its own right too. For the sponsoring company, embedding of learning also maximises ROI.

As well as time, there is also an investment cost in terms of budget from the sponsoring organisation. This is likely to be more than the investment required for a 'standard' sales training course, as more will be involved such as assessment fees (e.g. for marking of assignments) and certification fees. Internal training teams can be trained to deliver sales qualifications, but more realistically they are likely to be provided via an external supplier, which means there will be the consultancy cost of their time and expertise too.

> **Key thought: The most expensive training is the training that doesn't change anything. Cheap training that doesn't work is actually more costly than the more (so-called) 'expensive' training that does!**

The counter-argument to this though is that the key issue should be ROI, not cost, and if a more robust process results in a greater ROI then it is indeed an investment rather than a cost.

A further consideration which impacts on cost is the actual content of the qualification, since attainment requires the completion of a specific learning syllabus – so a given list of topics and subjects. If any one part of this is left out, the qualification is incomplete. *How* this syllabus is presented can be flexible; what the syllabus includes is not. This can mean that participants receive input related to a greater breadth of subject areas than they would if attending, for example, a bespoke and more highly targeted training course or training workshop.

An argument that's sometimes levelled against developing the sales team in any way, is that there is a danger that they will become so highly skilled that they become targets for competitors who want to head hunt already trained and talented sales professionals – often so they don't have to do this themselves. The logic of such companies is that it's better (easier!) to remunerate more highly than to spend money on sales training. But why should a salesperson want to leave an organisation just for more money? ...if that is, the current organisation provides ongoing coaching, supports personal development, and provides a working environment that's highly motivating and engaging? If the working environment isn't like this, then yes, there is good reason to move for just an increase in pay. The point is, the move isn't because of the training that's been received, it's because of a working environment that's not engaging or motivational – and that is (for the most part), influenced by the behaviours of the Sales Manager. So don't blame the training...!!

Key thought: One Sales Manager says to another: *"What if we train them and they leave?"*. **The other Sales Manager** replied: *"What if we don't and they stay?!"*

Realistically, I have seen one or two occasions when sales qualifications have accelerated the movement of an individual from their organisation. This has happened when a more senior member of the sales team or even the Sales Manager themselves has studied for a higher level qualification such as Diploma, Degree, or Masters Degree. Not surprisingly, the know-how acquired fires up enthusiasm to apply their learning, and to improve issues internally in order to drive enhanced sales results. This is all good of course... unless that individual isn't actually allowed to apply what they've learned, and unfortunately this can, and does, happen. It typically happens when the newly qualified individual has developed themselves to a level where they have greater know-how and expertise to their 'superiors' (note the inverted commas – superior in job title only!). However, instead of being allowed or even encouraged to apply what they've learned, they are held back and have to remain in the same role inputting in the same way as they were before attainment of their qualification - even though they probably now 'see' a lot more that they could do and help with than they did before (NB comments above regarding how sales qualifications change how you think). In short, they end up out-growing their organisation, and most certainly end up out-growing the line manager, who might even feel a bit threatened.

It's certainly true that when implementing what they've learned, the qualified individual should act with sensitivity, tact, and diplomacy in order they can indeed apply within the business what they want to. Even those most blessed with such ability though can find themselves being 'stone walled'. A pity, as they have the capability to bring so much extra to their role and to their employer. And again, the issue is not caused by the sales qualification, but because of the limitations of the more senior management within the organisation...

This also raises the issue of ensuring that those who work towards achievement of sales qualifications (at all levels) have realistic expectations regarding how attainment will impact on career progression...

I would recommend that a clear message is communicated that attaining a sales qualification does not automatically result in a promotion or change in job title or anything else. These things are earned via achievement of the right results, plus utilisation of the right behaviours in the business, plus the demonstration that they are the person with the most appropriate package of skills, knowledge and attitude for the role. It is true that sales qualifications provide the skills and know-how that enhance ability and so they can accelerate career progression. They are not the reason for any promotion though; the reason is the enhancement of abilities.

So realistically, the key drawbacks of sales qualifications are the amount of time required to study for them, the extra costs involved, and there can be issues around managing the expectations of participants. That's why sales qualifications are not a panacea for every development requirement. Having said that, when managed appropriately they do offer some interesting extra benefits to a standard training course or workshop.

Vocational Qualifications

Vocational qualifications are work based qualifications, which are awarded for demonstrating the application of the skills and knowledge required to complete the job successfully in a work-based setting. In the UK, there are recognised National Occupational Standards (NOS) for many different job roles, including of course sales. The NOS, are, in simple terms, a description of the pieces of skill and knowledge required in order to achieve success.

What makes vocational qualifications a little different to a 'standard' qualification, is that the list of competencies that need to be demonstrated is quite prescriptive, and objective evidence needs to be provided which demonstrates application of <u>all</u> of them. Any skills and / or knowledge which an individual is lacking needs to be provided via training. However, there is no absolute requirement for an individual to have any training at all if they already have all the skills and knowledge that are required for the qualification. A more experienced salesperson who has already received the necessary training, and who wants to gain recognition via a formal qualification in sales, simply needs to demonstrate application of the NOS in the workplace. A newcomer to the sales profession with absolutely no experience though will require the relevant training input as a precursor to demonstrating application of the NOS.

Demonstration of ability to apply skills and knowledge can be achieved via a variety of methods, including …
- …'live' observations
- …recordings of telephone calls with customers
- …role-plays
- …documented evidence
- …interviews by a qualified assessor to gain relevant evidence

203

Note that all of these examples are focused on the acquisition of objective evidence, which again is a little different to 'normal' qualifications which most often accept a written assignment as evidence of understanding and application.

So overall, the key benefits of vocational qualifications are that they are gained by (in simple terms) showing that you can do the job to recognised standards, and training is not compulsory – participants only need to be provided training to acquire the skills and knowledge they don't already have. The key downside is the amount of time and effort that's required to build the portfolio of evidence that's required in order to achieve the qualification, since this evidence needs to cover <u>all</u> the competencies of the qualification. Another plus side to them though is that there is no strict time limit on this, though clearly it's important to put a time plan in place in order to retain momentum.

In the UK, National Vocational Qualifications (NVQs) are available for many roles, including both front-line sales and customer service. Whilst they are relevant to all salespeople, they are arguably most appropriate for those in the early stages of their sales careers, who are in the process of learning the core know-how required to succeed in the role.

Professional Institute Endorsements

A kind of 'half way house' between simply providing relevant sales training and providing formal sales qualifications is to have the training that's provided to the sales team formally endorsed. Exactly what this entails will vary between countries and indeed between individual institutes. The following description therefore should be regarded as a 'typical example' rather than an accurate description of all endorsement procedures from every professional institute in every geographical location globally.

Endorsement means that a robust and formally recognised body, which will typically be a professional sales institute (for example the UK based ISM) 'badges' the training that's being provided as having relevant content which is being provided by appropriately experienced and qualified trainers, in a manner which is appropriate to the audience concerned, and to a recognised level of quality. This recognition will normally also provide some indication of what level of sales qualification the training is similar to. Participating delegates receive a certificate on completion of the training which is co-branded with both the logo of the organisation that's provided the training, and also of the endorsing institute. Since such certificates communicate that an individual has received training of a recognised quality, they are more meaningful than a simple 'certificate of attendance' which simply states that an individual has attended a given course. Equally though, the recognition is not as meaningful as a formal sales qualification which states that an individual has *demonstrated application* of what's been learned.

The main benefit of this approach is the co-branding of the certificates. This can be more motivating for the individual salesperson, and for the sponsoring organisation can help to brand their sales team as having received high quality training – which might both help to differentiate them in the market place, and might also help to attract high quality sales professionals into the business.

Another benefit of endorsement is that it doesn't necessarily require proof of application – so the cost and time of doing this is removed. '*Not necessarily*' though are two important words here... The awarding institute needs to be satisfied about the quality of the training only, and delegates are normally able to receive a co-branded certificate on completion of the training. It isn't compulsory though for the sponsoring organisation to take purely this approach. The sponsoring organisation is able, should it wish to do so, to add in additional requirements over and above the requirements of the institute.

The approach I always recommend is for certificates to be awarded only after application of learning has been demonstrated and/or measured in some way, and ideally when there has been a measurable impact on relevant KPIs. This drives a more robust development process, and makes the certificates and the awarding of them far more meaningful, and so more potent as a motivator. The process described in chapter 4. for linking KPI changes to recognition fits in with this approach very well.

Key thought: Institute endorsements should be used in the way that best drives achievement of the sponsoring organisation's objectives – and their format provides the flexibility which underpins the ability to do this.

A good example of this was a company in the pharmaceutical industry I enjoyed working with who were employing a new sales force for the UK. This organisation was focused in particular on key account management (KAM), wanted to ensure that all who were employed into this new team received robust and high quality training, and wanted to know for sure that they were applying these principles successfully in the real world of the competitive UK market place. Formal endorsement for the modular programme I designed for this team was successfully attained, and the UK Managing Director and myself wanted to ensure that this endorsement had real meaning and significance. Our vision was for the awarding of the certificates to be a potent motivational tool as well as a 'badge of quality'. So participating delegates were required to develop an Action Plan during the training programme, identify what KPI's successful implementation of the Action Plan would influence, and subsequently measure the changes that were indeed achieved (again, the process described in depth in chapter 4.) Certificates could then be awarded objectively measured business results which had been driven by meaningful training.

To repeat something mentioned above, this is a lot more meaningful than a simple certificate of attendance, particularly when certificates are formally presented by the Managing Director at a high profile, motivational, Awards dinner.

The drawbacks of endorsement are the costs involved, and the fact that endorsement relates to the quality of the training that's provided rather than what participants do with what they learn - though this latter drawback can be managed by using approaches as just described. There is usually a cost for the initial endorsement of the training programme, an annual renewal cost of this fee, and a cost for each certificate co-branded with the logo of the endorsing institute. It should also be noted that training programmes are endorsed on an individual basis, so the costs are per training programme endorsed, rather than a one-off cost for the organisation.

How relevant endorsement is to an individual organisation will depend on a number of factors including:

- How much more motivational this will be for participants.

207

- Culture of the business providing the training.
- Culture of the market place where the sales team operates.
- How much it will impact positively on customer perception and so company and sales team brand.
- Relevance / recognition of the brand of the awarding institute in the location(s) where the sales team operates, by both customers and the sales team themselves (endorsement from a UK sales institute may not be regarded as being of high relevance in other countries).

Because the process of endorsement is relatively simple, it is certainly an option which is worthy of consideration.

Membership of Professional Institutes

In the ever-evolving world of professional sales, and in a world where this evolution is, if anything, increasing in pace, it's essential for top performing salespeople to retain an up to date understanding of recent developments in the world of professional sales. Membership of professional institutes provides a means of achieving this.

Do note the generic reference to 'professional institutes' rather than purely 'professional sales institutes', as there are good reasons to consider membership of industry specific institutes as well. It's appropriate first though to consider the pros and cons of being a member of a professional sales institute...

The only downside of membership is the annual cost, though this should really be regarded as an investment rather than a cost, with the sales professional then being responsible for ensuring maximum returns from this investment are accrued.

In terms of benefits, membership normally provides designatory letters, the level of which will be dependent on experience and qualifications (e.g. ACIM, FCIM, i.e. Associate and Fellow of the Institute of the Chartered Institute of Marketing respectively). Some in the sales team will find this motivational, and addition of designatory letters on business cards, LinkedIn profiles, and other relevant literature certainly helps to communicate a brand of professionalism. Institute members normally also receive a journal or magazine (either virtual or hard copy) with articles which can be informative, provide an insight into leading edge thinking, or simply be a useful thought provoker.

The most significant benefits though relate to the provision of networking and educational opportunities. These can include..

- International conferences (e.g. those of the Global Sales Science Institute and the Strategic Account Management Association, see www.globalsalesscienceinstitute.org and www.strategicaccounts.org)
- National conferences – which can be one or more days and include input from leading thinkers in the profession, plus sometimes smaller break-out sessions which provide more of a chance to interact with these speakers (e.g. the annual sales conference of the APS, see www.associationofprofessionalsales.com).
- More local regional meetings – smaller, more intimate, often just a morning or evening.
- LinkedIn Groups specifically for members only.
- Training courses – often with discounts available for members.
- Webinars – often free, and again, specifically for members only.

- Member only resources accessible via the web site of the Institute (White papers, videos, articles, studies, etc.)
- Library facilities – both real and virtual via the Internet (e.g. the Chartered Institute of Marketing offers members on-line access to academic & business journals and articles, see www.cim.co.uk).

…hence the comment above: "…the sales professional then being responsible for ensuring maximum returns from this investment are accrued" – since taking maximum advantage of these benefits and utilising them to further develop knowledge, skills, and expertise, requires an investment of time and effort on top of the investment of the membership fee. Some institutes offer personal benefits too, such as discounts with retailers and service providers, and free access to a legal helpline.

As well as sales specific institutes, membership of industry specific institutes is worth considering. These provide similar benefits, but with a specific focus on industry specific issues such as…

- Product knowledge (e.g. advances in technology)
- Competitor product knowledge (e.g. new entrants)
- Industry trends (e.g. impact of globalisation)
- Changes in legislation (e.g. impact of changes in health & safety legislation)
- Trends in customer requirements & also buying behaviours (e.g. increased use of central buying points)

Again though, it's not so much the membership of the Institute that's important, but maximising returns from the potential benefits that membership provides.

Summary

The world of the professional salesperson is arguably more challenging today than ever before. It makes good sense therefore to ensure they are better prepared to address these challenges than ever before. Sales qualifications are an option or tool that can be used to achieve exactly this.

The word 'qualification' can be misleading, since it's more often than not associated with what we experienced when we were at school, which for the most part was probably theoretical. Sales qualifications though require students to demonstrate application, and so demonstration of how the student has used what they've learned to achieve a better result when doing the job. They are, in fact, very practical. Qualifications are available from Certificate through to PhD, and although not a panacea, they do provide the Sales Manager with more options to consider when *developing the skills of the sales team*.

Vocational qualifications and also professional institute endorsement are other tools that might help. They all have their place; like any tool, they need to be used when they are appropriate and in the way that best enables the goals of the sponsoring organisation and the Sales Manager to be achieved (or preferably exceeded!)

Membership of professional institutes offer a myriad of benefits; it's difficult to think of a good reason why anyone employed in professional sales would not want to be a member of certainly a sales related institute, and perhaps one or more industry specific ones also.

There is a cost in terms of cash resource for sales qualifications and institute membership, and a cost in terms of time for the successful attainment of a sales qualification. As discussed in chapter 4. ("Maximising returns from Training & Development"), the key issue isn't so much 'cost', but ROI. And as with everything related to developing the skills of the sales team, maximising ROI is about application in order to drive higher quality Inputs, which in turn will result in the achievement of higher quantity and/or quality of Outputs.

7. Developing the Sales Manager

Although all of the principles so far discussed in this book are just as applicable to the development of Sales Managers as they are to the other roles in the sales team, there other issues specific to the Sales Manager role that need to be considered over and above this.

It's always a good idea to have a pad and pen by the side of you when you're reading a book so that you can quickly make a note of thoughts, ideas and actions that reading provokes you to think about. For readers of this book who are already Sales Managers or who are aspiring to move to this challenging role, if there is ever a time to do this, then now is that time! In particular, as you're reading this chapter, keep the following three key questions at the front of your mind:
  1) How clear am I on where I want to take my career?
  2) How robust is the Personal Development Plan (PDP) that is taking me there?
  3) What more / different can I do to expedite my personal growth?

Me plc

The "Me plc" concept is about managing yourself and your career in the same professionally thought through way as you would a business. And fundamental to managing a business successfully is

213

to have a practical and pragmatic business plan which is focused on moving the business towards its Vision, is underpinned by thorough and robust analyses, and is routinely monitored and amended as required. A career plan should be no different.

I once heard a story about an aircraft flying long-haul from the UK to the United States... A few hours into the flight and part way across the Atlantic, it flew into a rather dark and gloomy cloud. Part way through the cloud, the aircraft was hit by a bolt of lightning. The aircraft shuddered a little and the lights in the cabin flashed on and off a couple of times, before it steadied and carried on smoothly towards its destination.

A few moments later, the captain very calmly made an announcement: "*Ladies and Gentlemen, you may well be aware that we've been hit by a bolt of lightning, but I want to reassure you that the aircraft is quite safe and our ability to fly has not been impaired. Additionally though, I have some good news but also realistically a little bad news as well. To get the bad news out of the way first of all, I need to tell you that the surge in electricity has damaged our navigation and radio equipment. I've no idea where we are or what direction we're travelling, and I can't speak to anyone in air traffic control to find out and they can't speak to me. BUT... I have some good news too. We've somehow picked up a really strong tail wind, and we're going to reach where-ever we're going really quickly!*"

And can't life as a Sales Manager be a little like that?! The job is demanding, and there normally isn't enough time in the working day and the working week to do everything that could be done. Very typically Sales Managers can be quite task focused, and are certainly goal and objective driven. It's little wonder then that it's all too easy to put on one side plans for personal development and career management in order to focus on the urgent 'here and now' activities which enable the Sales Manager to *achieve sales through others*. Prioritisation though is key! Board members of a successful enterprise would be expected to not only react to and manage the issues of the day, but to also strategically plan for the long-term well-being of the organisation, implement that plan effectively, and update and amend it as required. Sales Managers should adopt exactly the same philosophy for the management of Me plc. Of course it's important to do the things that will drive success today. There also though needs to be an appropriate focus on proactively managing the future.

> **Key thought: Sales Managers should have a business plan for "Me plc". Do you?**

"Me plc" – the Business Plan

A strong business plan begins with clarity regarding the Vision – the long-term, aspirational end-point, that is often so ambitious and so big that it's almost outrageous. It's surprising though just how often the Vision is eventually achieved, as once it's in place there is greater clarity about the activities which do and do not support successful movement towards that Vision.

So for Sales Managers reading this I need to ask: "*How clear are you on where you want to take your career in the long-term?*" This is not about the next job you will have, or even the job after that (be those moves within your current organisation or with different organisations). This is about the point that you will attain when you are at the pinnacle of your career. This isn't necessarily about wanting to eventually be CEO of a global business. If that *is* the case, then that's fine of course. For others though it might be to be recognised in the profession as the absolute top performing Sales Manager in the industry with the highest performing sales team in that industry. Or it could be to be one of the founders of a professional sales institute that raises the profile and levels of professionalism of the sales profession in your particular country. Or it could be to move into independent consultancy in order to be a 'trouble-shooter', who is parachuted in to organisations on a temporary basis in order to turn-around underperforming sales teams. It doesn't matter what the Vision is …what matters is *having* a Vision for Me plc.

To explain the importance of this very simply: it's very difficult to plan what route a journey is going to take, unless you know what the destination the journey needs to move you towards. Me plc is exactly like that; it's very difficult to put together a development plan and Action Plan which will move your career to the destination you want, unless you know what that desirable and wanted destination actually is.

Some reading this might argue that this isn't possible today, and that in the fast moving world of the 21st century, what's important is being nimble and flexible in order to make the most of any career opportunities as they arise. And this is true of course… the world is faster, and it is important to quickly make the most of opportunities as they arise. This doesn't mean though that there can't be clarity about the destination for the journey – where the ideal end-point is going to be. Having a clear Vision and making the most of opportunities as they arise are not mutually incompatible. Once there is clarity about the career Vision, then which of the opportunities that arise are and are not going to be helpful will be a lot clearer.

And isn't it also true that once it's been decided where the career path is heading, all of a sudden you begin to notice the chances and opportunities which are going to help?!

Realistically, there might be a change in the Vision along the way, and again, that's fine of course. Experience and an increased understanding of who we are and what our inherent strengths and aptitudes are, might change our understanding of what we are most suited for and so what we want to achieve. But the basic tenet remains the same... there should be clarity about where you are going to proactively take your career.

Key thought: If you haven't decided where you want to take your career, someone else will decide for you!

Going back now to the similarities between a business plan and the plan for Me plc... once a business is clear on where it aims to move to in the longer term, the next step is to consider what can help the business move in that direction, and what potentially might slow down or totally inhibit progress. Only then can an Action Plan be put in place to capitalise on what's helping, and to proactively manage what is or might in the future hinder progress.

The business plan for Me plc is no different. Once there is clarity about the career Vision, the next step is to complete a SWOT analysis – on Me plc. So very typically this would include bullet points similar to those in figure 18. Note that this includes a column for potential actions and doesn't simply list the factors that might be helping or restraining. The idea behind this column on the right hand side, is that as the SWOT analysis is being completed, ideas that come into mind about an Action that should be taken (to capitalise on a Strength or Opportunity, or to proactively manage a Weakness of Threat) can be quickly noted down and added into the plan. It's the identification, prioritisation, and implementation of these Actions which will proactively move the Sales Manager successfully towards their career Vision...

The outcome of such planning should be a series of Actions, preferably with timings, which will enable the entity known as "Me plc" to move successfully towards its Vision. That's the good news. The bad news is that realistically, this will entail more work and effort. But isn't it true that once it's been decided what the important activities are, then we tend to find the time to do them? The Action Plan for Me plc is no different, and the very fact that Actions have been thought through and identified means that they will become higher priorities, and so will indeed be implemented. All of which is very different to the Sales Manager acting like an aircraft not knowing where it's heading and with a strong tail wind... very busy and moving issues forward to achieve sales today, but without any sense of what needs to be done to move their career in the *right* direction. Then all of a sudden it's ten years later, and that person is in the same job doing the same things. Their more proactive colleagues meanwhile have all moved on to a variety of different roles and are well positioned to move on again towards the Vision that they have embraced.

OK, this might be an exaggeration! It is meant to be provocative though, and in particular to provoke thought. Everyone has just one career. Make sure your career is the one that you want it to be.

Career Vision

To lead a Global sales team to the achievement of the "Global Sales Team of the Year" Award at the annual Industry Sales Awards.

(current position: Regional Sales Manager, responsible for North and North-West of the UK)

Strengths * Proficiency in French * Track record of success	
Weaknesses * Lack of knowledge & experience in Change Management	* Acquire training input. * Gain involvement with project teams internally who are involved in proactive management of change
* Currently have a low profile in the Industry	* Speak at industry seminars
Opportunities * Institute representing UK industry	* Speak at seminars. * Active involvement on steering committee
* International sales conferences	* Attend. Network. * Potential speaking engagement.
Threats * Current employer might be purchased by competitor organisation	* Bolster portfolio of skills & experience. Be positioned on purchase as high profile and valuable.
* Downturn in market	* Network – extend number of contacts in other companies and in similar industries

fig 18. Some examples of actions driven from a SWOT analysis of Me plc

Mentoring, Buddying and Coaching

The second book in this series, "Sales Management: So now you're a Sales Manager…" considers the issue of mentoring in some detail. Suffice to say here that all of these tools support the development of skills, knowledge, know-how and confidence…

Mentoring …is about enjoying a professional relationship with someone who has more knowledge, experience and expertise than you have. The 'mentor' is someone who can provide input (so direction and/or training), can help provoke thought so the person being mentored (the protégé) can think things through (so coaching) and is someone who can provide practical advice and know-how. More-over, they are someone who the protégé can turn to and ask for advice, and sometimes even for a conversation on confidential matters.

When first appointed as a Sales Manager I was appointed a mentor who was one of the more respected and senior members of the UK Sales Management team. Hindsight being the exact science it is, I can see now that I should have utilised that relationship a massive amount more than I did.

Buddying …is similar to mentoring in so much as this is a sort of relationship between two people. The difference to mentoring though is that the other person (the 'buddy') is in a similar role, may well have similar levels of experience, and might also be at a similar stage in their career. They may be a colleague in the same organisation, or they might be external to the organisation. In this sort of relationship, they are there to help you, and you are there to help them; you are buddies, sharing experiences and problem solving together in order to navigate the challenges that the Sales Manager role provides.

These relationships can be particularly useful for more experienced Sales Managers, who have been incumbent in their role for a while, and want to avoid their thinking being confined to the environment they are in and are already familiar with. Buddying with a fellow Sales Manager from a different company and indeed a different industry can work particularly well in this scenario.

For someone who is relatively new to the role, both internal and external 'buddy' relationships can work well too; having an internal buddy can be particularly useful though, as you can then help each other understand internal issues such as policies and politics.

Mentoring and buddying are not mutually exclusive. It is possible to have both a mentor and a buddy at the same time. Whether or not such a comprehensive package of support would or would not be appropriate though comes back to the initial premise described at the beginning of this chapter – it's important to have clarity of Vision and an understanding of personal strengths and weaknesses related to that Vision in order to understand what the most appropriate Action Plan is.

Coaching …is (as discussed in some depth in chapter 3.) a potent method of provoking thought, and can most certainly be applied to the acceleration of personal development and career progression.

Coaching is one activity that might be included as part of a buddy or mentor relationship. Another option here is to hire the services of a professional coach, who might not necessarily be an expert in sales or Sales Management, but who does have a great deal of prowess and expertise in terms of coaching managers and leaders within businesses generally. These sorts of relationships can work well for the more

221

experienced Sales Manager; indeed, I know of a number of companies that encourage such relationships and provide the cash resource required to enable them to happen.

Ensuring that these relationships operate effectively requires there to be an understanding by both parties of what the purpose of the relationship is, and an agreement as to how the relationship is to operate. The first 'coaching' meeting is often focused on achieving exactly this, with it being as much a conversation as it is coaching; since the relationship is going to be a two-way thing, it's important that both the coach and coachee are happy about how the relationship is going to work.

The most important issue to clarify at this first meeting is the purpose of the relationship, and in particular the answer to the question: "What is this coaching relationship going to help achieve?" Clearly, the more specific and measurable the answer to this question is, the better; for example.. "Prepare the Sales Manager to successfully aspire to a National Sales Manager role within a three-year period".

For many relationships though, the purpose may be less specific than this, and be simply something like: "To support ongoing personal development". The second question that needs to be considered when embarking on the coaching relationship can help here, which is: "How are we going to measure ongoing success?". This question aims to provoke thought about the milestone achievements along the way, and the measurable outcomes which communicate that the investment of time and budget is providing the desired returns. For the earlier very specific purpose of achieving the National Sales Manager role, this would be about identifying all the building blocks that need to be in place for this ambitious goal to be realised. For the less specific purpose related to supporting personal development, this could be something like…

* …agreement to clear actions following each coaching conversation.
* …implementation of agreed actions.
* …identification of tangible positive impacts on career progression.

Understanding how to measure value from the relationship is a fundamental building block which should be put in place as the relationship commences. Indeed, how else can investment of the time and budget required be justified? The Sales Manager in the relationship would certainly want to justify the cash investment if it were their own hard-earned money rather than the company's!

Measuring value derived from the relationship is just as important for the coach too; they will want the person they are coaching to understand clearly the returns being accrued from the investment. This is important from an ethical and moral standpoint, and in terms of marketing is important since a happy and satisfied customer is more likely to provide referrals and introductions!

Some sponsoring companies will require that the budget provider is provided at least some feedback that a return on investment is being achieved. Others I have known take the view that they believe they have a responsibility to support personal development, believe that coaching is an effective support tool, and that the professional Sales Manager should simply be left to manage the relationship as they see fit in order to make it work and so maximise returns from it. Their ethos is that a requirement for the Sales Manager to monitor and report back over-formalises the relationship and so damages it. Whether or not feedback is provided to budget holders, I would argue it's good practice to always *be able to provide* that information if it were required, since this means that the coachee is always in a position to justify further investment... at the very least to themselves.

> **Key thought: Measuring the value of a coaching relationship is important for all stakeholders: the coachee, the sponsoring organisation, and the coach themselves.**

Feedback to budget holders which is definitely not appropriate are the specifics of what's discussed during coaching meetings. The most effective coaching relationships are those where the Sales Manager is absolutely, totally, 100% open with their coach about their feelings, worries, concerns, and perceptions. If it's suspected that information is going to be fed back to key influencers in the business, then this honesty and openness isn't going to happen. In short, the relationship simply isn't going to work. And it's important that there is an overt agreement regarding this between not only the Sales Manager and their coach, but also with other key stakeholders such as the Sales Manager's manager, and HR.

Admittedly, there are times when this agreed confidentiality should be breached, which are if the...

- ...Sales Manager being coached wants to share with colleagues the content of discussions and the coach is in agreement with this.
- ...Sales Manager being coached wants the coach to provide feedback to stakeholders within the business on a particular issue. Though if this happens, there needs to be clarity about what's going to be communicated and where any 'boundaries' lie.

- …coach needs to provide information to the sponsoring organisation in order to prevent injury to the Sales Manager or others, or to prevent or manage a breaking of the law. These though are *very* extreme circumstances!

As well as monitoring how well the relationship is providing value, It's also important to consider and agree how both parties are going to monitor how well the relationship is working generally. Essentially, this is about agreeing how feedback is going to be provided to each other. My recommendation is that this is candid, honest, and ongoing, and that there is an 'up front' agreement that such feedback will be listened to, discussed, and responded to accordingly. It's good practice to conclude each meeting with a discussion about how productive the conversation has been, what's worked well for both parties, and what improvements could be made. When the coaching relationship is working well, this conversation might only be a couple of minutes. This doesn't matter though; it's the principle of making this part of the standard process that's important. The principle of not making any assumptions is important too.

Should one party feel uncomfortable about an aspect of the relationship or how the conversations are being managed, then the agreement to provide candid feedback means that this can be raised quickly and with minimum feelings of discomfort. Once discussed, it's then down to the relevant party to modify their behaviours accordingly. The only reasons this would not happen are:

- If they are incapable of modifying their behaviours (and may or may not realise that).
- They could modify their behaviours but don't want to.
- They could modify their behaviours, are willing to, but fail to invest the effort required to do so.

All these three scenarios describe situations where the relationship is unlikely to work effectively anymore. Which also means that the point in time may well have come to draw it to a close...

Which brings us on to another issue: finishing the relationship. Sooner or later the coaching relationship will *have* to finish. This could be for a number of reasons, including because all the goals and objectives initially set have been achieved, budget may no longer be available, or one party may no longer wish to engage in the relationship. The fact remains though, that sooner or later the relationship will need to finish – be that for a very positive reason or a less positive one. Ironically then, it makes good sense when first beginning the relationship to agree on how it's going to end! So another important component of that first meeting which 'sets the scene' is a conversation about what could result in the relationship moving to a conclusion, and how both parties are going to manage that situation professionally. The conversation around being open with each other, and providing candid and honest feedback is important here.

I would also argue that the very intangible, but critical issue of 'chemistry' needs to be considered during that first meeting; does both the coach and the person who is to be coached 'feel' comfortable with each other, and 'feel' that the relationship is going to work? If that intangible 'chemistry' is not there, then it's better to agree there and then that the relationship is not going to work as well as both parties would like, and an alternative coach is probably a better option. Pressing ahead regardless is *highly* likely to result in the relationship struggling, failing, and coming to an end anyway – only time will have been lost, and there are likely to be bad feelings on both sides at that point too. That's not 'professional'.

Finally, some thought has to be given to operational issues – where and when will coaching meetings take place and what will be their frequency. Face-to-face meetings are obviously preferable to telephone since communication will be augmented by body language. The first meeting of the relationship which 'sets the scene' should most definitely be face-to-face (though it's recognised that sometimes even this might not be possible – for example when the coach is based in a different country or even continent). What proportion of meetings are face-to-face rather than virtual depends on lots of factors such as location, average meeting duration, depth of discussions, and the sensitivity of the situation being discussed. Where possible, virtual meetings should take place via a video-conference facility, such as Skype. Frequency of meetings depends on purpose of the relationship, but as a broad 'rule of thumb' there needs to be sufficient time between meetings to implement agreed Actions, but not so much that momentum is lost. I find a period of around 6 weeks works quite well.

> **Key thought: Board members and senior managers of very large organisations very often engage the services of a coach. If it's good enough for them, then it's probably good enough for the CEO of Me plc too!**

In summary, mentoring, buddying and personal coaching are all effective approaches to take in order that the Sales Manager enjoys accelerated personal development and career progression. These approaches though should not be embarked on without appropriate consideration. Which approach or approaches are most appropriate depends – on the Vision and analyses in the business plan for Me plc. Once the most appropriate approach(es) have been identified, then they need to be initially set up properly and then managed in a manner which is professional, will accrue the desired returns, and so provide a healthy ROI (of both time and cash resource).

For Sales Managers reading this, the key message is a simple one: You are the CEO of Me plc; it's up to you to ensure that you grow your business in the most effective way in order to achieve your Vision.

Business knowledge and awareness

Acquisition and/or bolstering of general business knowledge and awareness is an important component of the Sales Manager's personal development for a number of reasons...

For many B2B focused sales organisations, this knowledge and understanding will help the sales team to win sales. It's important to understand the needs of Decision Makers and Influencers in the customer's business; a broad understanding of the different business functions within a business will certainly help with this. It's one thing having a good understanding of your proposition and the advantages that it has over the competition… it's another thing though being able to articulate this information in a way that's meaningful, persuasive and relevant to the individual stakeholder. To be able to do this requires an understanding of their role, what Key Performance Indicators are likely to be used to measure their performance, and an ability to speak in their language. A Finance Director may well be interested in discussing how your proposition is going to influence Net Expense Ratios, Cash Flow and Liquidity ratios. A CEO may well be interested in discussing how your proposition is going to impact on Net Client Gains and

Return on Capital Employed. The key thing is to understand what issues are likely to be on their agenda, and to be able to use the right terminology in the appropriate way. And of course, once this know-how has been acquired, it can be passed on to the less experienced members of the sales team and future newcomers to the team too.

The same principles are relevant when selling internally. A key responsibility of the Sales Manager is to represent the sales team and influence internally in order to acquire support and any necessary resources. For example, part of the sales plan may include a recommendation that for the first time your organisation should actively support and sponsor a key industry exhibition. For this to happen successfully, the likelihood is that a number of colleagues will need to endorse and support the idea. The Sales Director first of all will require a robust proposal which describes how ROI will be maximised, what that ROI is expected to be (taking into account all relevant issues such as lost opportunity time), and how all this is going to impact on what they personally are measured on: sales results! Colleagues in marketing though might want different information such as why this activity is deemed to be more effective than other marketing related activities such as a more targeted approach, or an e-based campaign of some description. And if a further tranche of budget is required from Finance, then as well as measures of ROI justifying the investment, they are likely to require comfort regarding risk mitigation. So whether the investment in the exhibition is worthwhile or not is only part of the issue; *communicating* that it is worthwhile in a manner which is appropriate and so influences and convinces others will be critical too.

No doubt the Sales Manager expects their team to be sensitive to differing business and emotional needs when they are selling to external customers; it's not unreasonable therefore for the sales team to have these expectations of their leader when that person is selling internally on the team's behalf.

Acquisition of an in-depth understanding of other functions and the effective application of this know-how will benefit the Sales Manager's personal brand and standing in the company too. 'Personal brand' is about the perceptions that others have of you. It's intangible, and impacts on emotions… how others *feel* about you. But just because it's intangible and involves emotions doesn't mean that it's not important. In fact, the very opposite is true; it's all the *more* important because of this! A personal brand which includes perceptions that the Sales Manager has an unusually deep understanding of how other functions operate, that they have gained a high level of respect internally because of this, and that they are always able to make things happen as a consequence of this – is good news. Such a personal brand is likely to impact positively on how often the Sales Manager is asked to be involved in special projects (which will again support personal development), and will also position them favourably for more senior roles in the future – which might be with their current employer, or potentially a different one.

All of which moves us to the key question: How do you gain this level of knowledge and understanding? The short answer to the question is "training", which as discussed in chapter 3. is about 'putting in'. This could include activities such as:

- Attendance of relevant internal training courses. A course that's provided by many organisations for this purpose is "Finance for non-finance managers".

- Attendance of relevant external training courses. Professional bodies very commonly provide a range of courses which can be attended by both their members and other paying delegates. For example, the Chartered Institute of Marketing (CIM) in the UK provides courses such as "Fundamentals of Pricing", and "Introduction to Marketing Metrics and ROI", and the Chartered Institute of Purchasing and Supply (CIPS) "Introduction to Procurement and category management".

- Attendance of seminars with speakers who provide an insight into key roles. The Sales Performance Association (SPA) in the UK regularly enjoys input from speakers such as Senior Procurement Managers.

- Enrolment in Business School courses and qualifications.

- Participation in cross-functional teams within your own organisation. For example, when working for the Barclays Group, I was a member of a Senior Management Group which made the high level strategic decisions for one of the main Business units. This provided me with an enormous amount of learning regarding the needs and points of view of colleagues in HR, Finance and Risk (Underwriters).

- Participation on committees outside of work. As straight forward as it might sound, active involvement in Groups such as Parent/Teacher Associations can all help to broaden experience and expertise.

- 'Shadowing' of colleagues – which means simply being with a colleague in another function for a day or half-day in order to see exactly what they do, and to be able to engage in an ongoing informal conversation regarding why they are doing what they do, and the thought processes which drive their activities.

231

Strategic thinking

These two words describe the ability to think at a 'high' level, and to be able to see and understand what I would term *the full picture* ...by which I mean how a given action or decision can impact on the whole organisation and indeed external parties, what the effects might be in the medium and long-term as well as the short, and for decisions and recommendations to be driven by a robust and objective analysis of all the relevant data and information. In short, it's a different way of thinking to the more tactical focus of *achieving sales today*.

When I enjoy the privilege of working with students who are embarking on high level sales qualifications (so Diploma level and above), I always comment that whilst they will accrue a lot of benefits from the skills and know-how the qualification will provide, the biggest benefit they will gain is the one that's practically impossible to measure. Participation in a high level sales qualification changes the way that you think. Most students nod quite politely, and indeed most find this idea believable. That doesn't necessarily mean though that they understand what this means... at least not until they are approaching the end of the qualification. I always raise this subject with them again at this point, and ask them about how they feel about what I'd said when they first embarked on the challenging pathway of learning at this level. Absolutely 100% of the time I receive a categorical agreement that they now understand fully what I was trying to express.

I often have delegates remark how surprised they are at the way that they are now thinking; it simply wasn't possible to perceive or understand in advance the difference that studying at this level makes. Very much a case of 'you don't know, what you don't know'! If you have seen the movie "The Matrix" starring Keanu Reeves, you'll understand the meaning of how one delegate described this change in thinking. He said: "*It's rather like The Matrix and awakening and finally seeing the real world around you. It was there all the time, but you just weren't seeing it!*" Nicely put! That's exactly what I mean by achieving the ability to 'think strategically'.

> **Key thought: The same world is in front of Sales Managers both before and after they study for a high level sales qualification. Only afterwards they see more clearly what's truly there…**

In terms of how to move to this higher level of thinking, then all the activities listed in the last section are relevant. My personal opinion though is that the most effective way is to participate and successfully complete a high level business focused qualification. This includes sales qualifications at Diploma level upwards, and can also include other broad based business qualifications of similar levels.

Participation in these also provides the opportunity to network, work with, and mix with senior managers from other companies and industries. This in itself is enriching, can promote higher level thinking, and enable a broader base of general business knowledge to be acquired.

Summary

All the content of this book which is focused on personal development is as relevant to the Sales Manager as it is to everyone else in the sales team. Over and above these things, there are a few issues which justify particular consideration.

The concept of "Me plc" is helpful when developing a longer-term Plan of Action to move the Sales Manager to where-ever they want to take their career. Although that assumes they do know where they want to take their career, and gaining clarity on this issue is often the first important step in the process.

Like any business plan though, the plan for Me plc can change, which often involves relatively small additions and amendments, and sometimes large and significant ones. Sometimes even the Vision might alter slightly; it might even change totally. Remember though, if you don't decide where your career is going, someone else might decide for you!

Useful in terms of personal development is to gain a solid grounding of business knowledge and acumen. This can be used to help the sales team achieve sales today, as passing this information and know-how on to them can help them to understand the needs of external customers and to communicate with them in their language. In just the same way, it helps the Sales Manager to communicate and influence internally – and help to build the personal brand of 'someone who can make things happen'.

Developing yourself personally requires an investment of time and effort. The returns though are significant in terms of personal growth, career development, and personal satisfaction.

8. Personal Development Plans

Personal Development Plans – what they are

Personal Development Plans (PDPs) are precisely what the title describes – a clear Plan of Action to achieve the desired growth and development of a given individual. The development might be targeted at improving their ability to achieve in the current role, and/or prepare them in advance of a move to another role at some point in the future.

For example, a salesperson might have aspirations to move to a more senior strategic account management role from the role they currently have which is focused on managing smaller and more tactical accounts. It makes good sense to arm them with relevant skills *before* moving to the role rather than afterwards when they might initially struggle to adapt.

Or it might be that the sales process and selling environment is likely to change, because the organisation is going to change its strategic focus to one which is going to concentrate on different markets which have different requirements and purchase in different ways. Or it could be that external influences are going to bring about change, such as changes in legislation, for example. Whatever the reason, the key purpose of the PDP remains the same: to help achieve the desired growth & development for that given individual.

An example PDP can be seen in figure 19.

235

Development Goals	How are the goals going to be achieved? Who else needs to be involved?	Target date (for each step in the plan)	Achieved (✓)	How will you know you have achieved your goal? What impact will it have on the business?
1) Improve ability to identify needs of customers related to Product range 'X'	* Review training material on Questioning & listening skills' * Coaching by Sales Manager & observational feedback * Develop bank of questions to elicit customer needs and requirements (with help of F.Smith)	Feb Ongoing April		* Increase in opportunities to provide Product range 'X' solutions * Increase in sales of Product range 'X' related products & services
2) Improve ability to win appointments via telephone	* Identify role models within Team. Contact and gain insight into what works for them. * Develop qualification criteria to identify high potential prospects. * Coaching by line manager. * Attend "Winning Appointments via telephone" workshop (date).	March March Ongoing May		* Increase in number of appointments won * Reduction of telephone calls required to win each appointment * Increase in proportion of first visits that convert to a sale

3) Prepare for move to role in marketing	* Enrol in Certificate in Marketing local college evening class.	June	* Successful completion of assignments & exams.
	* Join Chartered Institute or Marketing & utilise reading and other resources.	Feb	* Verbal feedback to manager re key information acquired.
	* Arrange day shadowing marketing manager	March	* Debrief manager
			* Invited to apply for next available marketing role.

figure 19. An example Personal Development Plan (PDP)

> **Key thought: A PDP is a clear Plan of Action to achieve the desired growth and development of a given individual.**

The development of PDPs normally takes place as part of the annual appraisal process. It would be wrong though if this implied that PDPs should not further evolve or potentially even change altogether between appraisals. The role of the individual might change, or future potential internal opportunities might change – both of which could well mean that the PDP needs to evolve in tandem with these changes. It would certainly be nonsensical to invest time and resource in development activities that became of limited relevance and benefit because of such changes. It is reasonable to suggest though that a number of the goals in the PDP (particularly those related to long-term career development) will be achieved via the implementation of a long-term plan involving numerous and (hopefully) synergistic activities – hence the logic behind the plan being reviewed in depth annually.

The columns in the PDP are as follows...

Development Goals – a broad description of what the individual is aiming to achieve.

How are the goals going to be achieved? Who else needs to be involved? – the critical Plan of Action. Bear in mind that a way of learning that suits one person doesn't necessarily suit everyone in the sales team. Some people in the sales team might enjoy methodically working self-dependently, by reviewing learning resources such as video-clips and reading materials, and then completing exercises in order to apply what they've learned to their role and the real world they work in. Others in the sales team might prefer to learn via dialogue and debate with others. So this section is most definitely not a 'one size fits all'.

It's also likely that more than one activity will be involved; indeed, this is normally the case.

How will you know you have achieved your goal? What impact will it have on the business? - The first of these questions is about understanding how there is going to be an objective measurement that the development goal has been achieved.

For acquisition of knowledge, this can be achieved by demonstrating that information can be recalled, which could be via a written, verbal, or e-based test.

Skills are different to knowledge (as discussed in chapter 1.), and the only way to find out whether someone has a given skill or not is to observe them use it. Someone who wants to improve their key account planning skills, for example, will know the development goal has been achieved when they can develop a key account plan that satisfies all the requirements the organisation has for such a document, and also agreement by the National Sales Manager that the plan has been completed to a satisfactory quality.

Both of the above examples (one related to knowledge, the other related to skills), do not articulate though how the learning is going to impact positively on the business. This is about measuring outcomes, so what's going to happen as a consequence of applying learning. This is what the Kirkpatrick model describes as 'level 4 evaluation' (again, as described in chapter 4.) Including this provides a number of benefits: It makes the PDP more meaningful to its owner, it provides an objective measure of success and so an opportunity for

239

recognition (a key motivator), it justifies the investment required to reach this point, and it subsequently justifies further investment in the individual (since they have demonstrated their ability to provide a healthy ROI). Most important of all, this approach continues to communicate and reinforce the message that development is not about training courses… it's about developing specific skills and knowledge via a variety of means, and that 'success' is not about completing the development experience, but about *applying* what's been learned and **achieving more** as a consequence. As has been alluded to on a number of occasions in this book, all this is about developing a **growth culture** within the business.

Following on from the examples above, a potential outcome of enhanced knowledge might be an increase in the proportion of customer queries managed on a 'first time' basis, and a potential outcome of enhanced key account planning skills might be an increase in the number of opportunities identified proactively rather than responded to reactively. Neither of these outcomes are complex or difficult to measure. But aren't they important?!

Target date – a commitment for each step in the plan to have been achieved by a specific date.

Achieved (✓) – Some would argue that this column is superfluous, since it will be clear whether or not one, some, or all of the steps in the plan have been achieved. I argue the opposite! It's very satisfying to be able to put a tick in a column to show that something has been achieved, be that a tick with a pen or a virtual tick via a keyboard. It's a motivator for many salespeople too; they are, after all, typically achievement focused and so enjoy recognition. It might even be the case that the ticks are put in the column during the review meeting with the manager, which will heighten that sense of achievement and recognition. And of course if someone has enjoyed successfully completing relevant personal development and derived a sense of satisfaction from the achievement and recognition that's been gained as a consequence, then they're more likely to want to do more of the same in the future – good news for both them and their manager.

Who owns the PDP?

Answer: The individual who the PDP is for. It's as simple as that!

They are responsible for ensuring the PDP is relevant, is up to date, and for reviewing progress to ensure that the plan is 'on track'. In short, they are responsible for managing Me plc!

This doesn't mean though that the Sales Manager should not take an active interest, or that the Sales Manager doesn't have a responsibility to help, support, encourage and coach each person in the team as they develop themselves. In fact, quite the opposite. But it should be made abundantly clear that the person who has ownership of the plan is the person who the plan is focused on.

The degree to which the conversation about the PDP adopts a mentoring rather than coaching style depends on a number of factors, the principal one of which is the salesperson's level of experience. The greater the amount of experience a person has regarding a particular issue, the more the Sales Manager is likely to adopt a coaching approach and style, and the less experience the person has, the more the style is likely to swing towards mentoring.

'Experience' is not though the same as 'tenure'. Someone who has been a member of the sales team for a prolonged period of time might have new aspirations to move to a role which involves significant amounts of negotiation with Procurement specialists – an area they've not dealt with before. So whilst having high tenure with the organisation, they have low experience of this new challenge. And they might also have very limited, if any, knowledge about how to bolster their skills, knowledge and know-how of how to negotiate at this level. If the Sales Manager does, then a style that's more akin to 'putting in' rather than 'drawing out' might well be the most appropriate approach to helping the salesperson develop a robust PDP. It will probably be more appreciated by them too. Asking coaching questions they don't know the answers to, could prove rather frustrating!

But once the PDP has been developed, then it's that salesperson who owns it.

Identifying skills and knowledge relevant to the PDP

At fear of stating the obvious, the skills and knowledge that the PDP will provide are those that an individual is currently lacking! So these are the building blocks that when put in place, will help the person either achieve more in their current situation or prepare them to achieve in a future one. On some occasions these will be very obvious, for example a newcomer to the sales team who is in the early stages of their sales career and might want to develop their presentation skills and also increase their levels of knowledge about key markets they are involved with. Or for someone moving to a more strategic sales role, some key aspects related to sales planning.

There are times though that the development requirements might be less obvious, and for these occasions it can be useful to refer to checklists of sales competencies as a thought provoker and a provider of information. Any reference list should never be used as a tool to 'tell' the Sales Manager and the owner of the PDP what development is required, but to provide input to a coaching style conversation which helps the PDP owner identify for themselves what is best going to help.

As described in chapter 3., the National Occupational Standards in Sales (NOS) in the UK is one such 'checklist'. The NOS provide a description of the skills and knowledge required in order to succeed in professional sales. They are not organised under specific sales roles, rather under broad subject areas such as 'Use sales technology systems for sales activities', with a more detailed description under this heading of what people need to be able to do in this subject area, and the skills and knowledge required to enable them with this ability.

A more 'rough and ready' approach that can be taken to provoke thought regarding development needs is the TNA tool shown in figure 6. and discussed in chapter 2.

For those who are planning to move to a different role in the same organisation, an up to date job description could be a useful source of information too.

Keeping the PDP realistic

Two main issues arise here…

The first of these is time. Whilst it's important for each person in the sales team (including the Sales Manager) to have a PDP, achievement of this plan happens *as well as* achieving the sales objectives of the role, not *instead of them!* Of course, if the PDP is helping to put the right skills and knowledge in place, this will contribute to the salesperson's ability to achieve anyway. It's also clear that supporting an employee's personal development contributes positively to levels of motivation and engagement, which will also impact positively on achievement. The key issue is that the Sales Manager continues to reinforce that the salesperson is primarily responsible for achieving the goals and objectives of the role, in just the same way as they would if they were independent agents and were, quite literally, managing Me plc. A self-employed salesperson with a professional mindset would certainly focus on self-development in order to ensure they were able to sell and earn more in the future, and that would be *as well as* earning a living today, not instead of it.

The second main issue is availability of internal development opportunities and budgets. Even within the very biggest organisation, there won't be sufficient of either to satisfy the potential development needs of every employee within the business. Indeed, for the larger organisations this challenge is even more of a headache as they tend to have more demanding employees! Having more demanding employees is a good thing, since it's an outward sign that a culture is in place where employees understand the need for personal development, are taking ownership of their PDP, and are seeking the input required to achieve it. But it does cause issues in terms of demand! There are two approaches to managing this…

Firstly, the Sales Manager needs to ensure that each person in the team has realistic expectations of what is, and is not, feasible and realistic. So the coaching conversations which support the initial development of the PDP and its ongoing implementation need to ensure that these realistic expectations are communicated effectively. The fact there are limited resources can also be used to reinforce the importance of successful PDP implementation, and in particular the objective measurement of outcomes which benefit the business, since this will help to justify further requests for resource (and in particular budget) in the future.

Secondly, the Sales Manager needs to help each salesperson, where possible, to source highly cost-effective or even free resources. The key people to consult here is the training team within the organisation, and in particular (if there is one) the sales training specialist.

(NB the discussion in chapter 5. regarding the evolving role of the training specialist, and the increased emphasis on 'curation'.)

If there is no internal training resource that can help provide this information, then other sources of help include the Sales Manager's networks and on-line self-help Groups such as the numerous Sales Manager specific User-Groups on LinkedIn. If you haven't already put a request on a LinkedIn Group for help do try it – you'll be amazed at both the number of responses you receive, and the quality of them.

> **Key thought: a new Sales Tip is posted on the highclere channel of YouTube every month – see**
> **https://www.youtube.com/user/highcleresales**

Summary

A PDP is a document which provides clarity about what's going to happen in order to provide the relevant skills and knowledge which enable a given individual to grow and develop. The purpose of this development might be to increase their ability to achieve in their current role, or to help prepare them for a different role in the future. The PDP provides clarity about what growth is going to be achieved, how it's going to be achieved, when it's going to be achieved by, and ideally also the benefits to the business.

It's the responsibility of the Sales Manager to help each member of the team develop and implement successfully their PDP. It's the individual salesperson though who owns it.

9. What can go wrong – and how to avoid these things

I've been in the privileged role of full-time sales consultant and trainer for over 15 years, so have now worked with an enormous number of sales teams from plenty of different industries. The various clients I've worked with have faced different challenges, and are involved in quite different selling scenarios (though the one common thread is that they are all B2B focused). This breadth and depth of experience has provided me with a good understanding of what makes development initiatives really successful.

Equally, I've heard about organisations who've either not achieved the expected returns from a development initiative, or failed spectacularly to achieve anything at all. I've also met quite a few organisations like this (though this was the situation before I commenced working with them I hasten to add!)

The stark truth is, that to implement development initiatives **in**effectively, you don't need to do anything complex or complicated! The things that cause the problems are normally simple and easy to understand. And as they are easy to understand, and because they can be proactively managed, an equally stark truth is that for the most part, disappointments and failures from development initiatives are avoidable - which is what makes it all the more upsetting when initiatives go wrong.

> **Key thought: the stark truth is that for the most part, disappointments and failures from development initiatives are avoidable**

Since the outcome of development activities is a more highly skilled sales team, capable of achieving a greater quantity and/or quality of sales Outputs, and since this impacts positively on the Sales Manager's job purpose of *achieving sales through others*, these are all issues that the Sales Manager should be interested in influencing. As with many issues though, this does not necessarily mean that it's the Sales Manager themselves who takes the necessary actions to manage them; there are many colleagues and other people who can help, not least of whom are the internal training team and/or any external partner consultancy who might be involved. It does though mean that the Sales Manager should understand these issues in order that they can ensure that they *are* proactively managed.

This final chapter of input from this book considers some of the very common things that can go wrong, and more importantly, what should be done to proactively manage these things if they do happen. Or even better, prevent them from happening in the first place. Many of the solutions to the issues described have already been discussed in other parts of this book. So this section can be regarded as being a reiteration of these solutions, and examples of practical application of these principles...

No buy-in from the sales team

This can happen when the entire sales team is going to be engaged in an internal training course, or training workshop, or indeed any other initiative. It can also happen when one or more individuals have been selected to attend an external event of some description.

Assuming that the development event has the content which will help the sales team achieve more in their role, it might seem strange that there's the possibility that they don't buy-in to what-ever is being provided. But this can happen. Reasons for this include:

- The sales team **perceive** that the content of the initiative *is not* relevant.
- Previous experiences have been less than positive – perhaps because the content of other events was not as relevant as it should have been (fuelling the above perception), or the facilitator may not have been a good fit with the culture of the team or simply not sufficiently highly skilled and/or experienced to deliver the event effectively.
- An external training course is being implemented internally, and there has been no tailoring of the content to the specifics of the organisation. Which means that any negative perceptions the sales team might have regarding the content of the event may be well founded!
- One or more members of the sales team have simply been directed to attend without any supporting discussion.

All of these reasons can be easily managed. So they should be!

For events which are designed specifically for the organisation and/or sales team, I recommend engaging with those who are recognised by the team as 'senior', and so are peer leaders within the Group. Share with them the goals of the initiative and its design. Ask for their input and guidance... after all, they are the most qualified of the team to act as mentors. And do then act on their input, and show them how the design has been amended and influenced as a consequence. With the ease of communication today, if peer leaders feel positive about the event that's being organised, then the rest of the team will soon know and are likely to feel the same way too. The same would be true of course if the peer leaders feel less than positive – which is why it's important to engage them in the process.

> **Key thought: Involving the 'senior' members of the team in the design of any initiative also acts as a means of recognition, which we know influences positively levels of motivation.**

Using the more experienced as mentors will also ensure that the content of the initiative is indeed pertinent and relevant – so a very practical output over and above winning the hearts and minds of key stakeholders.

Once the design and content is right, then as described in chapter 4. ("Maximising Returns from Training & Development"), it's also important to involve everyone who's going to attend in some pre-event activities. A live webinar is an effective tool I often employ for this. The webinar is not simply provided for the sake of it, but provides useful and relevant information that is of value to the participants, and is linked to the purpose and content of the event.

Providing information in advance also saves time during the event itself, and so liberates time for high value activities such as Group exercises, discussions, and problem solving. The pre-event webinar can also 'set the scene' for what the event is going to include, and most importantly communicate the benefits for those who are going to participate. It's also ideal to set one or more tasks to be completed before attending, with a requirement for the outputs of these tasks to be brought to the event. In essence, this means that delegates are already working on application of what the event is going to provide even *before* attending.

At the very least, joining instructions should be sent in advance which describe the purpose of the event, its content, and provide clarity about how the event is going to help those attending. There is no reason why delegates can't be asked via this document to complete one or more tasks in advance in just the same way that they can be on conclusion of a webinar. And there's no reason why the peer leaders who've helped fine-tune the initiative design and content can't be recognised and thanked in any covering correspondence.

The pre-briefing meeting with the Sales Manager plays a key role too, as was described in chapter 4.

A lack of buy-in to an external event by one or more individuals in the sales team is normally caused by a lack of pre-briefing by the Sales Manager. If the salesperson knows why they have been selected to attend, the KPIs that the event is going to help them to influence positively, and how they are going to be coached and supported by the Sales Manager afterwards to implement what they learn, why *wouldn't* they be enthusiastic about attending?! It would be even better if the Sales Manager has helped them to identify a number of development options and then

251

select the one that's most appropriate for themselves, rather than attendance of an event being presented to them as a *fait acomplis*.

This straight forward package of measures should manage pretty well all the reasons listed above which can lead to a lack of buy-in. And to repeat an earlier statement: *"All of these reasons can be easily managed. So they should be!"*

No buy-in from the Sales Management team – to the course

This most typically happens when an initiative is implemented internally, be that via an external partner or via colleagues from the training team. And it most typically happens when Sales Managers perceive that the initiative is going to provide no or limited value – but is going to take the sales team away from what they are employed to do: sell!

This potential scenario should be proactively managed by engaging in similar activities to those which win the buy-in of the sales team, namely involvement of the Sales Management team in advance of the event, as well as the pre-event involvement of specific representatives of the sales team themselves. Provided that there is clarity about the KPIs the event is going to positively influence, how these KPIs are going to be positively influenced, and the potential returns that the required investment of time and effort is going to accrue, then it would be a very strange Sales Manager who would remain ambivalent about supporting the initiative.

No buy-in from the Sales Management team – to the process

This is a situation that does arise far more often than it should; it's the situation where the process that's described in chapter 4. ("Maximising Returns from Training & Development") is not followed very enthusiastically, if at all. As a consequence, attendance of a development event by one or more of the sales team is not followed-up enthusiastically, and the Sales Manager therefore is not as aware as they should be of the specific actions that the participating salesperson(s) have listed on the Action Plan they developed during the event. Follow-up support and coaching is, at best, spasmodic... if it happens at all. It's all very much a case of the sales team being left to do everything for themselves.

Since Sales Managers who are reading this by definition do care about *developing the skills of the sales team*, then this section is arguably superfluous! It is important to broach this subject though, as even today it is still encountered from time to time.

There is no easy answer to this though. This is not just a failure of Sales Management... it's a cultural failure within the organisation as a whole. And the very big problem with cultural issues, is that they take a long time to shift. Change in culture is normally small-step and evolutionary, rather than radical and evolutionary. Cultural shifts don't tend to happen due to an immediate action or two, they tend to happen as a consequence of a sustained focus on what should be the right behaviours. So if the wrong development culture is in place, then the likelihood is that it's been in place for a long time and is ingrained. It isn't going to change overnight.

The most potent influencer of cultural evolution in this scenario is the manager of the Sales Managers, who will normally be the National Sales Manager or Sales Director. For the culture described above to be in place means this person does not believe that it's important to pre-brief salespeople before they attend a development event, or to coach and support them afterwards as they implement their Action Plan. If they did, then they would invest more time and effort to gain an understanding of how well their Sales Management team did these things. And of course, the old adage 'what gets measured gets done' is very true... if the Sales Director begins to measure how well their managers are maximising returns from investment in training & development in this way, then there is a strong likelihood that these things will be done more often. The primary challenge in these circumstances therefore must be to 'sell' them the idea, and of course the best way to sell anything is by communicating the benefits, which in this case is how this approach will impact positively on achievement of the sales plan.

Persuading, convincing, influencing, and changing how someone perceives such an issue is going to be long-term and strategic, rather than short-term and tactical. The following though will help:

- Demonstrating objectively that the Sales Managers who are adopting the right approach are achieving more, and achieving these things more quickly.
- Utilising respected external Influencers. For example, persuading the Sales Director to attend an external conference which is going to discuss this issue. Or asking a mutual contact (who the Sales Leader knows and respects) to communicate key messages on the subject.
- Taking every opportunity to remind and reinforce that this is the approach that's adopted by the more successful sales

organisations (see the Case Studies provided in this book for two examples!)

At the same time as aiming to influence the Sales Leader, it's also a good idea to build 'islands of excellence' within the Sales Management team, by which I mean supporting and encouraging those Sales Managers who have an interest in this area. There is no doubt that those who do adopt the right approach to maximising returns from development events, will indeed enjoy greater levels of benefit. When they see that they are accruing more benefits, then this is likely to become self-perpetuating. And of course the more that this happens with the more enlightened of the Sales Management team, the more objective data there will be which shows that this approach isn't just theoretically right, it's pragmatically and profitably right too.

As I say though, if you're a Sales Manager and you're reading this, then I'm proverbially preaching to the converted anyway! So these comments are aimed more at internal training specialists who are working in such environments, and who want to make a difference to the long-term success of the organisation.

Lack of budget

Budget is a precious resource, and any sensible organisation will utilise this precious resource wisely – which means focusing on ROI. Hence, the usual reason that budget is lacking is because there is a lack of objective data regarding what returns have been accrued in the past. Again, there is a detailed discussion about this in chapter 4. Suffice to say that my own opinion is that for far too long, the benefits of appropriate investment in the development of sales teams has been measured very subjectively, if measured at all. And that's why we have this situation all too often today.

Also worth considering are the comments in previous chapters about the wealth of free resources that are available today, and the evolving role of the training specialist towards more of a curator role, than one which designs training events and materials, and so potentially re-invents the wheel. It's always worth questioning what different options are available to provide the skills and/or knowledge that are lacking in order to ensure that budget is indeed being used effectively. Sometimes access to free resources just might do the trick!

Inappropriate use of on-site facilities for development events

Using the organisation's own on-site facilities rather than hiring external ones is likely to save money, so this can be a sensible approach to take. There are even some circumstances where this is not just appropriate, but highly beneficial to the achievement of the goals & objectives of the development event, for example…

- …in the lead up to a new product launch when a visit of the factory enhances the content of the event.
- …when there are purpose-built facilities, which might include video-recording facilities, telephone training equipment, etc.
- …to enable sales teams who are normally field based to network with head office based colleagues.

However, it is also true that if used inappropriately, on-site facilities can reduce the effectiveness of development events. Examples of this would include:

- When one or more participants meet with colleagues during coffee breaks, which detracts from their focus on the objectives and content of the event. Worse is when they 'quickly' meet at their colleague's office away from the main training area and arrive back to the course late. Now they've lost part of the content of the event, and also disturbed the learning of others.

- When the Sales Manager has a 'crisis' and pulls one or more of the delegates from the course to 'quickly' sort the issue. Not only does this terminate the learning of those who are removed from the event, it also affects the experience and learning of others, particularly if the ability to implement successfully team exercises and group debates is damaged. More-over, by doing this the Sales Manager is communicating two very negative messages: 1) Developing the sales team is a low priority, and 2) Leaving the event both mentally and physically is OK.

- The environment the on-site facilities provides is not conducive to a high quality development event; for example, if temperature control is inadequate, or furniture and other facilities are badly worn or damaged.

Again, the solutions to these are in the control of the Sales Manager... For the first on the list, the Sales Manager simply needs to be clear on what the 'rules' are, and to role-model the behaviours that are expected. For the second, the same comments apply; the Sales Manager wouldn't remove participants if the event were being implemented off site, so why should they when it's implemented on site?! And for the third, the most expensive development event is the one that fails to achieve its objectives; appropriate investment in an external venue here is most definitely the way forward!

The wrong external partner is being utilised

The easiest way to prevent this situation is to ensure that the right partner has been selected in the first place, the *right partner* being the one which provides support which is aligned to the all the principles that have been described in this book. Fortunately, a good proportion of sales consultancies these days do provide exactly this sort of support. So over and above this, consideration can be given to which potential partner best fits the culture and style of the sales team and business they will be working with.

A summary of some of the key issues to consider is provided in Appendix 2. This can be used by the Sales Manager themselves, and passed on to any colleagues in the training team and/or Human Resources who are involved in the selection process.

Summary

There are, no doubt, an enormous number of issues which can prevent training & development from being implemented effectively. It tends though to be the same few reasons that crop up over and over again.

Some of these relate to the culture within the business. Some relate to how the process of training and development is being implemented. What they all have in common though is that to a greater or lesser degree, they happen because of what the Sales Management team and the Sales Leader(s) within the business do. Hence the easiest fixes are to change what the Sales Management team and the Sales Leader(s) do!

So without apology, it's worth finishing by repeating what was said towards the beginning of the chapter:

"The stark truth is, that to implement development initiatives *in*effectively, you don't need to do anything complex or complicated! The things that cause the problems are normally simple and easy to understand. And as they are easy to understand, and because they can be proactively managed, an equally stark truth is that for the most part, disappointments and failures from development initiatives are avoidable…"

10. Overall Summary

Sales Managers are not employed to train salespeople. They are employed to produce results, and these results are of course about achieving (or preferably exceeding) the sales plan. After all, the purpose of Sales Management is *to achieve sales through others.*

It's critical though that the sales team are armed with the knowledge, skills, and know-how which will drive success. Sports teams provide a useful analogy here. Even the most talented individuals train hard to retain their level of success; it's tough to get to the top, and of course it's even tougher to stay there. At the other end of the spectrum, apprentices need to be instructed on what 'best practice is – what's been learned via practical experience produces the results. And then they need coaching and encouragement as they take on board, utilise, and develop these skills. And grow both in ability and confidence. Sales teams are not greatly different.

That's why it's important for the Sales Manager to understand how to develop the skills of the sales team. Not necessarily because it's them that does everything. Some activities certainly are their responsibility, coaching and developing a growth culture within the business being the obvious examples. They can though also call upon the support and services of others such as internal training specialists and external consultants. Making the most of these opportunities though means that the Sales Manager needs to have at least an understanding of the key principles that underpin effective Training &

Development. And that's what this book has aimed to have provided.

Utilise the following checklist to ensure that you are indeed doing what's needed to *develop the skills of the sales team*...

Checklist for Success

Sales Manager Input / Activity	Yes	Partly	Not sure	No
I take into consideration the differing requirements of different 'generations' when arranging development events.				
All my team understand that 'development' does not equal a training course! And sometimes means simply learning by doing the job,				
The sales team are provided Training & Development driven by a robust TNA, not by a list of available courses.				
Training & Development is targeted where-ever possible to positively influence specific KPIs.				
I have attended a quality course which has provided me with professional coaching skills.				
I practically always adopt a coaching style of management, only moving from this approach when it's justified to do so.				

Sales Manager Input / Activity	Yes	Partly	Not sure	No
Any feedback I provide is based on objective observations of behaviours, and avoids subjectivity.				
I routinely ensure that we understand which KPIs that are going to be influenced by any development activity, and when possible measure these both 'before' and 'after'.				
We have a clear process in place when preparing for, implementing, and following-up development events – in order to maximise ROI.				
I measure objectively ROI, and routinely publicise the impressive returns we achieve from investment in the organisation's resources.				
I always help each person in the sales team to review ALL the options available to address their development needs, taking into account personal preferences as well as cost-effectiveness.				
We always consider as an option, use of sales qualifications and other similar approaches when considering the most appropriate way forward.				
I encourage my colleagues in training to act as 'curators' rather than re-invent material that's already available, and provide them guidance on what my team requires.				

Sales Manager Input / Activity	Yes	Partly	Not sure	No
I network outside my organisation, am a member of a professional sales Institute, and make the most of relevant development opportunities the Institute provides.				
I have a robust PDP.				
Each person in my team has a robust PDP.				
I enjoy a productive and motivational meeting with each member of my team about their career aspirations at the very least once annually.				
We proactively manage all the issues that could potentially lead to a lack of buy-in to a development event or cause other problems that reduce effectiveness of development initiatives.				

Case Study: "Situational Selling Skills" - Hilti GB

Introduction

You may have come across a saying related to sales results in a growing market: "All ships go up on a rising tide"; in other words, it's very easy to increase sales when the market as a whole is growing anyway.

The environment Hilti GB (Hilti) was operating in during 2012 was rather different to this. The country was in the midst of a recession, and the construction market the company sells to fell in size (potential sales value) by 11%. Buyers were arguably more cautious than ever before. The products that Hilti was selling meanwhile, were premium priced – two or even three times the cost of their competition. One might expect a fall in sales of 11% in line with the market to have been acceptable, if not an achievement – particularly as Hilti's sales the previous year had been a record high. *Actual* results though were staggering – sales continued to **increase**!

This Case Study is the story of how this success was fuelled, which was principally by the introduction and implementation of a new selling skills programme: Situational Selling Skills (3S). Hilti already had an effective selling skills programme in place; 3S was a new and updated programme designed to address specifically the needs of the customer and environment of 2012. Not surprisingly, the initiative won the 'Best Sales Programme' category of the 2012 TJ Training Awards (created and organised by the magazine 'Training Journal', the TJ Training Awards recognise excellence in Learning & Development).

The content of this Case Study is based on an interview with Nigel Biscombe, Develop & Coach Manager for Hilti GB, plus a morning observing 3S first hand (both were carried out in January 2013), along with the content of the entry form for the TJ Awards.

Hilti – A brief overview

The Hilti Group is a worldwide corporation which manufactures and sells tools for the construction, property maintenance, and mining industries. Hilti's product range is extensive, and includes products such as drills, cutting tools and installation systems. The company's head office is in Liechtenstein, and employs globally over 20,000 people, with around 60% of this number in a sales role of some description.

The company sells direct to the End-User, which makes it different to a lot of its competitors who sell via distributors and retail outlets. Customers can buy on-line, by visiting a 'Hilti Centre', through telephone based customer services, or directly from a Hilti account manager, who can visit and demonstrate tools 'on site'.

The business is focused on providing high quality, and this ethos spreads across products, services, and customer interactions. Hilti's strapline describes its products well: "Hilti. Outperform. Outlast." When an opportunity to develop a new offering is identified, two key questions are asked. The first of these is: "*Can we develop a product which is significantly superior to the competition?*". If the answer to this question is "*yes*", then the second question asked is: "*How big is* the potential market?". This second question is important, since developing new and superior offerings means that the product will be more costly to develop, and the cost of research & development needs to be recouped.

The implications to selling are clear; Hilti needs to be able to articulate how its products provide value via superior performance and lifetime value, rather than by their initial cost as their competition can do. For account managers who visit the customer on site, telephone based customer service personnel, and the Hilti Centre staff, this means in turn that they need to have the skills which will enable them to do this.

3S – its development

'Situational Selling Skills' evolved from 'Strategic Selling Skills', which in turn had evolved from 'Strategy for Successful Selling'; so it was in fact the third in a series of 3S programmes. "*3S had been running in some format for over 20 years*", explained Nigel, "*and we aimed to retain the 3S logo for continuity. The new full title though conveys well the requirement of today's market; one size does not fit all – we need to understand the specific situation, challenges and needs of the individual customer, in order that we can present knowledgeable information, in order that they are able to make an informed decision.*"

Whilst the Hilti sales team was already successful, it was recognised that the world that Hilti's customers were operating in had changed, which meant that the way they thought and purchased had changed too. There was a requirement therefore to evolve the way that Hilti sold in concert with this.

To understand what was required, Hilti first conducted extensive research. This involved interviewing salespeople and managers globally, benchmarking Hilti's approach to other companies, industries and professional training practices, and gaining feedback from customers via questionnaires, interviews and focus groups.

As a consequence of the research, Hilti identified 24 critical sales competencies that underpin success. One of the other interesting findings was that the majority of learning / sales training is actually achieved via field based coaching, mentoring and training by the Regional Manager (the figure quoted was that 76% of all learning is achieved in this way). This finding underlined the critical importance of engaging line management in the design, implementation and follow-up & embedding of the new 3S.

"*Head office retains overall ownership of the programme, since it's important that we achieve global consistency, and that what each MO* (Marketing Organisation – each individual subsidiary) *does communicates and demonstrates to both new employees and customers our four Core Values of Courage, Integrity, Teamwork and Commitment. However, it was the responsibility of myself and my training team here in the UK to 'localise' the programme with specific examples related to our market and culture, gain the buy-in of line management, and ensure that 3S was implemented as an ongoing development initiative rather than just a stand-alone two-day course.*"

3S - implementation

"*Before we were able to implement the programme, it was first of all piloted centrally by a selected group from the sales team*", Nigel explained. "*Thanks to their feedback, the content, running order and style of the course was further fine tuned before it was introduced to MO's globally, including us here in the UK.*

Myself and Dan (Dan Stringer, Advanced Training Scheme Trainer for Hilti GB) *chose to initially run 3S here in the UK with the Regional Management Group. This was going to be critical to success – partly because they were able to populate the course with real examples specific to the UK, but mostly because this would mean that they would take ownership of the programme, embrace the concepts, terminology and language, and reinforce all this during field based coaching – which is their activity four days every week. The initial research had reinforced just how important field based coaching is, and we were keen to ensure that this became an ongoing initiative to further develop the culture of the business – not just a new two day course. Moreover, the Sales Directors attended and participated in the course with the Regional Managers too – which demonstrated clearly their commitment to the initiative, and their expectations of how the Regional Managers were to reinforce the principles.*"

The entire UK sales team attended a 3S course during 2011 and into early 2012, whether they had attended an earlier version of 3S or not; the initiative was focused on ensuring that the entire team was selling 'the Hilti way' rather than providing an optional bolstering of selling skills.

The training though involves more than just the two days of the actual course... "*Delegates are required to complete pre-course e-learning. This is good practice logistically because it frees up time when we're together for more productive activities. It also though engages minds in advance, and enables us to begin to communicate one of our strong principles, which is that it's the learner who is responsible for maximising what they gain from any development opportunity. As a company, we put our people at the core of everything we do, and so we provide enormous support for people who want to develop themselves. At the end of the day though, it's down to them whether they maximise this opportunity or not.*"

The actual two-day course itself is a risk-free learning environment which is rich in its variety of approaches and media in order that it appeals to all learning styles. Apart from PowerPoint – which is not used at all. So the course includes presentations by delegates in teams (to validate the pre-course e-learning), group discussions, individual exercises, group exercises, and role-plays. Nigel explained: "*We don't shy away from role-plays or the terminology. It's important for people to be able to rehearse and practice the skills the course develops. But the way we do it is to slowly build up each component of the face-to-face discussion before providing an opportunity to rehearse and practice the whole thing. The other thing that's important is to emphasise that this is an opportunity to practice, get wrong, and correct; we don't expect people to get it absolutely right first time.*"

When the Regional Managers attended the course, not surprisingly they were also provided with guidance on how to better coach when working with their team members. Interestingly, input on coaching, what it is, and how it benefits the coachee is also provided to the sales team when they attend: "*The logic is two-fold. First of all this increases the salesperson's appetite for* coaching, and so supports the Regional Manager. Secondly, it provides ideas about how to 'self coach' when working on your own, which of course will be the situation for most of the time the individual is actually selling. So again, what we are aiming to do is to build up a sense of personal responsibility."

3S has also become now a standard part of the induction programme, being routinely days 4 and 5 of the first week of employment. As with the initial roll-out of the programme, newcomers to the sales team are required to attend and participate fully whether they already have selling experience and have attended other sales training or not. The requirement is to ensure that everyone knows 'the Hilti way'. "*The whole of the induction is about ensuring people understand, are aligned to, and will live our values. Having said that though, we are very careful about who we employ in the first place. Of primary importance is to establish whether they can wear 'the Hilti jacket' – is it a good fit or not? There is a certain sort of person who fits the Hilti culture, and not everyone is a good fit with our values. If the Hilti jacket doesn't fit, then it doesn't matter if you can sell or not, you're not the sort of person who we want in the team. Now this doesn't mean that you're a bad person, but it does mean that you're not a Hilti person.*"

Follow-up

As described earlier in this Case Study, Regional Managers work four days each week with their team – an ideal opportunity to coach, support, and reinforce 3S principles. To help with this activity, the UK training team developed a coaching template which the Regional Management team could use as a 'checklist'. "*Undoubtedly*", commented Nigel, "*this has contributed very significantly to our success*."

Regional Managers also use Regional meetings to revisit and reinforce 3S principles, and to recognise successes achieved via its successful implementation.

The training team also follows-up with 3S participants directly, gaining feedback at 3, 6, 12, 18 and 24 months after attendance of the course. The aim of this activity is to understand which parts of 3S are of most value, and what further evolution, if any, is required. Questions are for the most part qualitative rather than quantitative, for example:

- "How well has the training helped?"
- "How well are you supported?"
- "How effective is the product training?"
- "How effective is 3S?"

"*Historically we've done this via e-mail with the questionnaire as an attachment. We're in the process though of moving to an on-line survey tool which will provide us with an analysis of the data automatically*", Nigel explained.

Results

When the new version of 3S was first implemented, the average growth achieved across all Regions globally was +14% It's important though to emphasise that this figure is not growth of 14%, but 14% *extra growth* over what was being achieved before the new 3S programme was rolled-out.

In the UK, in an extraordinarily price sensitive and cautious market which was decreasing in size, sales increased – and increased compared to the previous year which had been a record. And again, it should be emphasised that this was with high quality products, which provide excellent lifetime value, but are far from the cheapest to invest in initially.

Ongoing sales development

Hilti has already introduced a more advanced programme as a follow-up to 3S. Entitled "Advanced Training Scheme" (ATS), this has been mapped against the UK National Occupational Standards in Sales by the Institute of Sales and Marketing Management (ISMM). As a consequence, those who complete ATS receive a Level 3 Diploma – a formal sales qualification they can retain for the rest of their career. The certificates are co-branded with Hilti and ISMM logos.

"We're in the process of developing a more structured and rigorous training programme for our management team on coaching. We know that the majority of learning is achieved via experience and line manager input, and that coaching contributes significantly to motivation and engagement. Coaching is also strongly aligned to our belief in Hilti about personal responsibility, since it's all about helping people to think things through for themselves rather than them being told. So the initiative on coaching we're aiming to launch later this year is good for our culture, good for the sales team, good for sales managers since it will enhance their skills set, and ultimately good for the business as it drives sales success."

Summary

3S won the 'Best Sales Programme' category of the 2012 TJ Training Awards because it was a lot more than a 'standard' training course...

The content first of all was borne from robust and rigorous research of the market place Hilti operates in. This research identified 24 specific competencies that underpin success, and the two-day course provides these skills and know-how. In other words, 3S is a bespoke selling skills event specific to the world of Hilti – or perhaps it would be more appropriate to say 'to the world of Hilti's customers'.

Learning is achieved via a large variety of activities and media in order to appeal to all learning styles. This includes pre-course e-learning, and post-course activities including sessions during Regional meetings. It's particularly refreshing though to note the total absence of PowerPoint!

Of critical importance though was winning the buy-in of the Regional Management team and their managers, the Regional Sales Directors. This not only helped to populate the programme with UK specific examples and content, but also ensured they were engaged in coaching and embedding the behaviours the course develops. The training team also provided the Regional Managers with some initial training on coaching skills, and provided 3S specific templates to support coaching activities. Hilti recognises this skill as so critical to their success, that a more in-depth and advanced coaching programme is currently being developed, and will be in place later in 2013.

Underpinning all of this though are Hilti's values, which include their people being put at the centre of all they do, and a high focus on the customer. What I learned from my time meeting Nigel Biscombe and observing 3S is that these Values are not simply words on a piece of paper as 'Values' can (sadly) be with some organisations; Hilti's values are lived by, and drive thinking & behaviours within the business.

The passion within Hilti to help employees grow is almost tangible. But employees are not spoon fed; there is a strong culture of personal responsibility. That's part of being a Hilti person, and part of what Nigel meant I believe when he referred to finding people who can 'wear the Hilti jacket'. It's not easy to become a Hilti person - not only because the company is highly selective, but because staff turnover is low; employees don't want to leave.

So this Case Study is about a lot more than a training course; it's about a business with a culture of personal growth, support, and a passion for quality – in terms of the products it provides and how it goes about doing these things. And it's a story about a business that's making success happen.

Case Study: "Developing Sales Team Excellence" - Merial UK

The following Case Study is based on an interview conducted in December 2011 with Tony Jones, Learning & Development Manager for Merial in the UK and Ireland…

Merial is the animal health division of Sanofi, selling products to veterinarians, pet owners, farmers and food animal producers worldwide. In the UK and Ireland the sales teams comprise of around 60 people.

Merial's UK sales success can be measured objectively by its consistent achievement of sales goals and objectives. There is also external recognition of sales excellence – in particular via successes achieved at the British Excellence in Sales & Marketing Awards (BESMAs) of the Institute of Sales & Marketing Management (ISMM). In 2011 Merial won the BESMA category "Sales Professional of the Year", having also won this same category in 2010, when they achieved both runner-up and third places too.

Successes of this stature are not borne from just one aspect of sales management. For example, it's important to ensure the most suitable people have been recruited in the first place. This Case Study though focuses on the structured way that Merial has grown the skills of the sales team – what the structure is, how it was developed, and how the sales management team (and not just 'Training') is engaged in its implementation. Not necessarily because Merial have discovered anything revolutionary or different to do; rather, that Merial understands exactly what best practice is, and has implemented this 'best practice' with consummate professionalism. They are an excellent example that other sales organisations would do well to emulate...

The Case study begins in 2005, when Nigel Slater became the new Head of Sales of the UK pet division of Merial. The sales team was expanded by 100% creating 3 Regions, with 9 Territory Managers in each reporting to a Regional Sales Manager. It became apparent that the organisation required a dedicated National Sales Training Manager. Prior to this, the sales teams were by no means poorly skilled or lacking ability to sell; but there was clearly an opportunity then to co-ordinate the skills, abilities and know-how that Regional Managers, technical experts, and mentors passed on to the sales team. Tony Jones was appointed to the role of Learning and Development Manager, having previously been in the Role of Regional Manager for the North of the UK.

The very first thing Tony did was to look at the needs and objectives of the sales force. This he did in conjunction with the Head of Sales, Nigel Slater; whatever was to be done needed to help the objectives of the business. Using this process would help achieve the buy-in of salespeople and sales management alike – something which Tony believes is "...*an important contributor to the success we've had*".

Prior to designing any training plan, the first obvious question to always ask is: "*What do our salespeople need to be able to do, and what in particular do they need to be good at in order to succeed* ?", and answering this question was indeed Tony's starting point. The job descriptions for Merial's various sales roles were the first port of call in obtaining the answer.

However these only provided a broad description of what salespeople needed to be able to do; there was a realisation that a more specific description of the actual competencies was required.

Rather than develop Merial specific competencies independently, Tony set up a meeting with members of different sales teams so that *they* identified what these competencies were; this again both facilitated buy-in, and ensured that the resulting competency descriptions were practical and fit for purpose. This was a critical step in the process, since the Output was an easily understandable description of what salespeople need to be able to do in order to excel in their role. Training could then be specifically targeted to provide precisely these things – some of which were areas of knowledge (e.g. competitor, business), and some of which were skills (e.g. questioning and listening, rapport building).

Armed with a much better understanding of what the ideal complement of competencies should be, sales managers were then able to assess individuals against clearly defined competencies and skills. This lead to the identification of specific training needs via both field based observations and any one-to-one reviews with their team. The outcome was a list of development requirements specific to each salesperson. This process is now ongoing rather than a simple once yearly review.

Tony's role was then, and indeed remains today, to facilitate the input required to satisfy these development requirements. This could be in any combination of the following methods:
- Via the series of 20 specifically designed modular courses which provide the full complement of competencies Merial has identified underpin success. These are bespoke to Merial, and are organised into five

stages, each of which builds on the previous one, with four of modules at each of these stages. All of these are designed internally. Each module has clearly defined outcomes and objectives and training delivery method. Some are implemented internally, and others by specialist external consultancies. Sales managers have provided input into the course design to ensure that content is practical, pragmatic, and specific to the world of Merial – and their involvement has further increased buy-in.

- Field based coaching by the Regional Management team. All sales managers received training in coaching skills and their application in a structured manner during field visits. The quality and quantity of field based coaching activity is measured and encouraged in a coaching style by Merial's UK Head of Sales. As already mentioned, active support of senior management has been a key contributor to success. Field based coaching is also recognised as an essential activity when following-up and embedding the skills learned during formal training events (as above).

- Coaching and mentoring by experienced members of the team. *"For the more experienced, this provides recognition of their expertise, acts as a motivator, and provides them greater challenge and more interest in the job"*, explained Tony. *"But coaching and mentoring are not haphazard or unstructured. We ensure the coach is very clear on the competencies that need to be developed, and also that the salesperson is equally clear on what competencies he or she wants to develop – which drives ownership of their personal development. What also helps are our Driving Principles and the Merial High Performance*

> *sales cycle. This is very clear and so constantly referred to during these conversations.*"

* Structured 'on-job' training.

* Reading and research on the Internet.

* Attending external seminars. Tony networks extensively outside of Merial, and in particular via the UK Sales Performance Association, which helps keep him abreast of relevant external opportunities.

Another important component to Merial's success in growing salespeople is *the overall mindset* of the approach. This is more about the *overall development process* (and in particular follow-up and embedding of what's learned) rather than just about the training course in isolation. Tony explained: "*We operate an 'accreditation process'. This means that six to eight weeks after attending a given course, the salesperson has to present to a team of managers and demonstrate to their satisfaction that he or she has understood the concepts that have been taught, that they have applied them practically, and that they have achieved more as a consequence. This is not an exercise in catching people out; it's about providing recognition of achievement! We have had people fail first time around, but this is only natural, in which case the process enables us to identify what help is needed. We provide a certificate for attending the course, but a more important one for accreditation. This sends a clear message that training is serious, and it's the salesperson's responsibility to embrace the opportunity to learn and grow. And all this helps to drive a healthy return on investment.*"

Overall, Tony believes there are some key elements of Merial's approach which have contributed to the significant successes achieved via training and development. These are…

- ...gaining the full and unequivocal support of the UK Head of Sales.
- ...identifying specifically for Merial what competencies are required to drive success.
- ...engaging the sales management team as a whole in the process and in particular in the creation of the competency framework.
- ...a robust accreditation process.
- ...effective follow-up coaching by the line management team.
- ...designing and delivering training modules with clear and measurable outcomes.

It's notable that this list does not include the content of the training modules themselves. This reinforces some of the key messages of this book related to the importance of approaching development of the sales team as a process rather than a training course, and in particular the importance of follow-up to embed skills and know-how learned.

It isn't surprising to find out that Merial has a very low turnover of staff in the sales team – role clarity, coaching, and the practices this Case Study describes are all recognised as drivers of engagement within a business.

Tony finished what was both a fascinating and motivating interview by making another observation: "*We now have people wanting to join Merial and the sales team because they have heard about our success at the BESMAs, and how we develop salespeoples' skills and abilities. Indeed, this has also been their motivation to try to leave their current employer – since they just don't do the same. Our development pathway means that right from Day 1, we can provide each individual with a document which provides absolute clarity about what they need to be able to do to be successful, and how to acquire the support required to further develop any skill areas that* *need to grow. Clearly, this is not only contributing to our ability to achieve sales, but to Position ourselves in a competitive employment market as <u>the</u> Organisation to work for".*

Appendix 1. Some useful coaching questions...

Goal

- What exactly would you like to discuss / solve?
- What's the issue?
- What do you ideally want to achieve / make happen?
- What do you want us to achieve today?
- What point do you want to reach by the end of this session?
- What needs to happen in order that you can leave and feel that this has been a really good use of time?
- If you had a magic wand, what would you really like to see happening (in the long term / as a result of this session)?
- What do you want to see / feel / hear happening differently?
- How far do you want to go as a consequence of this session?
- What is the long term objective?
- What is it reasonable to expect to achieve in the shorter term?
- What outcome would be of highest value to the Team?
- What ideally should they be doing differently?
- What ideally should be happening differently?
- What does 'success' mean in this context?

Reality

- What's happening at the moment?
- Who else is involved?
- How much do others impact on the situation?
- What other priorities do you have?
- What else influences this?
- How often does this happen?

? When does this happen?
? What tends to prompt this to happen?
? What impact does this have on you / the Team / the business?
? How accurate is your perception?
? What data objectively supports your beliefs?
? How much influence can you have (in the short term / long term?)
? How long has it been like this?
? How do others see the situation?
? What's been done to fix it so far?
? Who else has tried to influence it before?

Option

? What can you do to change the situation?
? What wouldn't work well in this situation?
? What has worked well in similar situations in the past?
? What could you do that you haven't done before?
? What resources are available internally / externally that might help?
? What are all the options for moving issues forward – no matter how fanciful (at this stage)
? What alternative actions can you take?
? Why might that one work?
? Why might that one not work?
? How would that impact on the situation?
? What's good about that idea?
? What are the pro's and cons of the ideas you've come up with so far?
? Pretend for a moment that you did have the answer – what would it be?
? How can you influence others to become involved?
? Who else might be able to help?
? Which of these options do you think / feel would work best?

? What support will you need along the way?
? How will you manage all the people who need to be involved?
? What could be the challenges and issues this solution causes?

Will

? So how will you feel when you get there?
? What will be the principle benefits to you / the Team / the organisation?
? How well does this solution achieve the objective(s) you identified?
? How is this going to be scheduled in the diary?
? What do you need to do to ensure everyone involved is on board?
? How are you going to ensure that the project achieves its timelines?
? What are you going to do to keep things on track?
? What contingencies do you need to put in place?
? What other resources might you need to support the solution you've selected?
? How confident are you now of success?
? How are you going to monitor progress?
? What will tell you that "success" has been achieved?
? What criteria can be used to measure success?
? What will be the first steps to take?
? What will be the easy and quick wins?
? What bigger and longer term issues should you begin working on now?
? What would you like everyone to feel when the objective is achieved?
? What are you going to do to celebrate success?

Adapted from Whitmore, J. (2009). *Coaching for Performance (Fourth edition)*. London: Nicholas Brearley

Appendix 2. A checklist to use when selecting an external consultancy to support development of the sales team

The most expensive training is the training that fails to achieve its objective(s); that's why the cheapest can be the most expensive! It makes good sense therefore to ensure you work with suppliers who will achieve the desired outcomes in the most cost effective manner. When differentiating between potential suppliers, consider the following:

Do they aim to provide bespoke programmes to your requirements rather than 'off the shelf' solutions?	**Yes / No**
Do they invest time to understand your business, language used, culture of your company etc.?	**Yes / No**
Are all the above used when designing and implementing the training event?	**Yes / No**
Do they provoke thought on other alternative solutions to ensure that a training event *is* the most appropriate and effective option?	**Yes / No**
Do they aim to identify specific KPIs that will provide a measure of success before proposing an intervention?	**Yes / No**
Do they aim to measure those same KPIs afterwards to measure success of the initiative and potentially provide a measure of ROI?	**Yes / No**
Do they encourage the Sales Manager to meet with delegates before the event?	**Yes / No**
Do they offer to provide pro-formas to support the above meetings?	**Yes / No**
Do they encourage the Sales Manager to meet with delegates asap after the event?	**Yes / No**

Are high levels of participation encouraged throughout the event?	**Yes / No**
Do they encourage delegates to identify and record the actions they are going to take as a consequence of attending the training event?	**Yes / No**
Do they aim to work with you to reinforce key learning from the programme afterwards?	**Yes / No**

References

(1) United Kingdom. Chartered Institute of Personnel & Development. (2015) *Developing the next generation – today's young people, tomorrow's workforce*. London: cipd.

(2) United Kingdom. Institute of Leadership & Management, and Ashridge Business School. (2011) Great expectations: Managing generation Y. London: Institute of Leadership & Management.

(3) Bristow, D., Amyx, D., Castleberry, S.B, & Cochran, J.J (2011). A cross-generational comparison of motivational factors in a sales career among gen-x and gen-y college students. *Journal of Personal Selling and Sales Management.* 31 (1), pp. 77–85.

(4) Kolb, D.A. (1983). *Experiential Learning: Experience as the Source of Learning and Development*. New Jersey: Prentice Hall.

(5) Kumar, V., Sunder, S. & Leone, R.P. (2015). Who's Your Most Valuable Salesperson? Havard Business Review, Vol 93. Issue 4, p62-68.

(6) Science of Ingagement. A report investigating the science of engaging employees, grounded in science, not fiction. (2014). Retrieved from Weber Shandwick Web site: www.webershandwick.com.

(7) Harter, J.K., Schmidt, F.L., Agrawal, S. & Plowman, S.K. (2013). The relationship between engagement at work and organizational outcomes. Downloaded from http://www.gallup.com/services/177047/q12-meta-analysis.aspx 14.5.16.

(8) Piercy, N.F. (2000). Field Sales Management Effectiveness and Performance. General Findings of the 1999-2000 SALES MATTERS Research Study. Cardiff.

(9) "IIP – Why Bother?!". Presentation by John Wrighthouse, Head of Group Training and Development, Nationwide. At Wessex branch of the Chartered Institute of Personnel and Development, 12th December 2005.

(10) Dixon, M. & Adamson, D. (2011). The Dirty Secret of Effective Sales Coaching. Downloaded from https://hbr.org/2011/01/the-dirty-secret-of-effective 26.5.16.

(11) Hubbard, J. (2014). Good Coaching Leads to Improved Sales Results. *ABA Bank Marketing & Sales*, Vol 46, issue 9, p12-13.

(12) Whitmore, J. (2009). *Coaching for Performance (Fourth edition)*. London: Nicholas Brearley

(13) Nohria, N., Groysberg, B. & Lee, L. (2008). Employee motivation: A powerful new model. Harvard Business Review, Vol 86, issue 7/8, p78-84.

(14) UK Commission's Employer Skills Survey 2013: UK Results. Downloaded from https://www.gov.uk/government/uploads/system/uploads/attachment_data/file/303495/ukces-employer-skills-survey-13-executive-summary-81.pdf 13.7.15

(15) Kirkpatrick, D.L. & Kirkpatrick, J.D. (2006). *Evaluating Training Programs: The Four Levels (Third Edition)*. San Francisco: Berrett-Koehler Publishers Inc.

(16) Olivero, G., Bane, D. & Kopelman, R.E. (1997). Executive Coaching as a Transfer of Training Tool: Effects on Productivity in a Public Agency. *Public Personnel Management*, 24 (4), p.461.

(17) Mehrabian, Albert (1981). *Silent Messages: Implicit Communication of Emotions and Attitudes* (2nd ed.). Belmont, CA: Wadsworth.

(18) Driving Performance and Retention through Employee Engagement. (2004). Retrieved from Corporate Leadership Council Web site: http://www.corporateleadershipcouncil.com/CLC/1,1 283,0-0-Public_Display-115966,00.html

Printed in Great Britain
by Amazon